THE GAME NIGHT COOKBOOK

THE GAME NIGHT COOKBOOK

Snacks, Noshes, and Drinks for Good Times

BARBARA SCOTT-GOODMAN

The Countryman Press

An Imprint of W. W. Norton & Company
Independent Publishers Since 1923

For information about permission to reproduce selections from this book, write to
Permissions, The Countryman Press, 500 Fifth Avenue, New York, NY 10110

For information about special discounts for bulk purchases, please contact
W. W. Norton Special Sales at specialsales@wwnorton.com or 800-233-4830

Manufacturing by Versa Press
Book design by Allison Chi
Production manager: Devon Zahn

Library of Congress Cataloging-in-Publication Data

Names: Scott-Goodman, Barbara, author.
Title: The game night cookbook : snacks, noshes, and drinks for good times / Barbara Scott-Goodman.
Description: New York, NY : The Countryman Press, An imprint of W. W. Norton & Company,
    Independent Publishers Since 1923, [2022] | Includes index.
Identifiers: LCCN 2021057191 | ISBN 9781682686942 (cloth) | ISBN 9781682686959 (epub)
Subjects: LCSH: Snack foods. | Cooking. | Cocktails. | Games. | Entertaining. | LCGFT: Cookbooks
Classification: LCC TX740 .S354 2022 | DDC 641.5/3—dc23/eng/20211122
LC record available at https://lccn.loc.gov/2021057191

The Countryman Press
www.countrymanpress.com

A division of W. W. Norton & Company, Inc.
500 Fifth Avenue, New York, NY 10110
www.wwnorton.com

10 9 8 7 6 5 4 3 2 1

For my dear friends and family,
thanks for the fun and games!

CONTENTS

CHAPTER 3
Breads, Bruschetta & Sandwiches

CHAPTER 4
Desserts & Treats

CHAPTER 5
Cocktails & Drinks

INTRODUCTION

In these often complicated and challenging times, many of us are thinking about how gatherings with our friends and family are evolving. We're taking stock of the relationships within our circles and realizing that intimate home parties are ultimately more fun and meaningful than meeting up in public spaces; they allow for curated hosting and deeper connections. We're also keeping our get-togethers lively by playing board games, creating home theater experiences, hosting binge-watching parties, and inviting people over for card nights, mahjong games, and many other activities.

It has been said that a lot of games were invented for groups of people who had to be around each other and were bored—like families. While that may be true to some extent, we all seem to have very fond memories of playing games (crazy eights and Sorry! in my house) with our siblings and neighborhood kids for hours on end. While some people think that playing board games, card games, and other games may be a thing of the past, we still take great pleasure in rolling dice, dealing cards, and moving our game pieces around the squares on the board with our buddies. Perhaps that's why game nights have become a thing.

One of the most important aspects of hosting a game night is figuring out what food to serve—because no matter what the occasion or activity is, we're all going to want something delicious to eat. While it is easy and convenient to open a few bags of chips and a prepackaged dip or two, you can create some tasty dishes with fresh and distinctive flavors instead. *The Game Night Cookbook* is here to help.

The recipes in this book raise the quality of everyday party food to new levels, and they're meant to be prepared with an easygoing approach that is sure to make any kind of occasion stress-free and a lot of fun.

This book features a number of new and original recipes as well as ones that are adapted from traditional ones. I remember my mother baking trays of Chex Party Mix for her weekly bridge club, and an updated, spicier version of that beloved snack is included here. Plain popcorn is given an Italian twist, and it's prepared like cacio e pepe pasta. The same goes for a creamy onion dip, which is made with fresh roasted onions, shallots, and thyme instead of dried onion soup mix from a box. There are recipes for homemade pizza with suggestions for scrumptious toppings, as well as ideas for creating and customizing luscious tacos that your company will love. If you want to assemble first-class cheese plates and antipasto platters, there are some excellent ideas and tips for putting them together. Playing games at the table usually requires some handheld food (that's how and why the sandwich was invented), and chapter 3, which features bread, bruschetta, and sandwich preparations, will come in very handy. In addition, there are recipes for heavenly desserts like lemon pound cake, blondies, brownies, biscotti,

and ice cream sundaes. There are also recipes for refreshing cocktails, such as kir royales for an elegant party, and mint juleps to sip on while watching the Kentucky Derby. A number of tasty non-alcoholic drinks and simple syrups that enhance the flavor of all types of drinks are featured as well.

The Game Night Cookbook is filled with good and practical ideas for making it all come together. I've included suggested menus that are perfect for lively, good-time occasions, such as the Game Day Buffet and A Swanky Evening at Home Cocktail Party. Follow these menus or use them as suggestions that inspire you to create your own style of party. All good hosts and cooks know that timing is everything, so each menu is accompanied by a game plan that is designed to maximize your schedule for prepping food and setting up, so that everything will be ready to serve when the time is right. These menus will help you plan ahead, entertain with ease, and make sure that you don't miss out on any of the fun.

There was a time when entertaining was a "should do" thing, but today it's done because we want to. Getting together with friends and family for fun and games along with good food and drinks has become a playful and enjoyable part of our lives. So put out the snacks, pop a cork, roll the dice, deal the cards, and play!

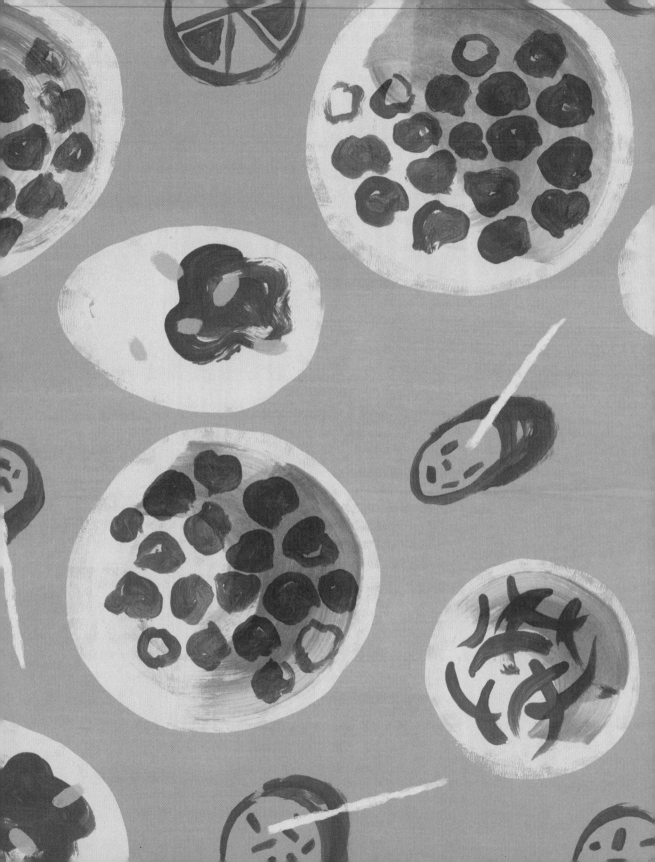

CHAPTER 1
SAVORY SNACKS & NOSHES

MAKES 4 CUPS

1 cup unsalted almonds

1 cup unsalted cashews

1 cup unsalted pecans

1 cup walnuts

2½ tablespoons unsalted butter

2½ tablespoons brown sugar

2 tablespoons chopped fresh rosemary

1 tablespoon chopped fresh thyme leaves

Pinch of cayenne pepper

Kosher salt and freshly ground black pepper

MAKE AHEAD:
The nuts will keep, covered in an airtight container, for up to 1 week.

Herbed Bar Nuts

This salty, crunchy snack is made with fresh herbs and a hint of brown sugar. These disappear fast, so you may want to double the recipe.

Preheat the oven to 350°F.

Put the nuts in a large bowl.

Melt the butter in a small saucepan over medium heat. Add the brown sugar, rosemary, thyme, and cayenne pepper and cook, stirring, until combined, 2 to 3 minutes. Pour the mixture over the nuts and toss to coat thoroughly. Season with salt and pepper.

Spread the nuts out on two large rimmed baking sheets and bake for 10 minutes. Toss the nuts with a spatula and continue baking until lightly toasted, about 5 more minutes. Remove from the oven, season the nuts with salt and pepper and let cool, 10 to 15 minutes.

Sweet & Spicy Roasted Nuts

Corn or canola oil for
  brushing baking sheets

2 cups unsalted pecans

2 cups unsalted almonds

1 egg white

2 teaspoons chili powder

1 teaspoon ground cumin

½ teaspoon ground
  coriander

½ teaspoon ground
  cinnamon

½ teaspoon cayenne pepper

2 tablespoons sugar

Kosher salt and freshly
  ground black pepper

These toasted nuts are so good to nibble on with a beer or a cocktail. They can be made up to a week ahead of time, so you can keep plenty on hand.

Preheat the oven to 350°F. Lightly oil two large rimmed baking sheets.

Put the nuts in a large bowl.

Beat the egg white in a small bowl until foamy. Pour the egg over the nuts and toss to coat thoroughly.

Combine the chili powder, cumin, coriander, cinnamon, and cayenne pepper in a small skillet and cook over medium heat, stirring constantly, until fragrant, about 3 minutes. Remove from the heat and stir in the sugar. Season with salt and pepper.

Add the spice mixture to the nuts and toss well to coat thoroughly.

Spread out the nuts on the baking sheets and bake for 15 minutes, shaking the pans every 5 minutes. Remove from the oven and let cool, 10 to 15 minutes.

MAKE AHEAD:
The nuts will keep,
covered in an
airtight container,
for up to 1 week.

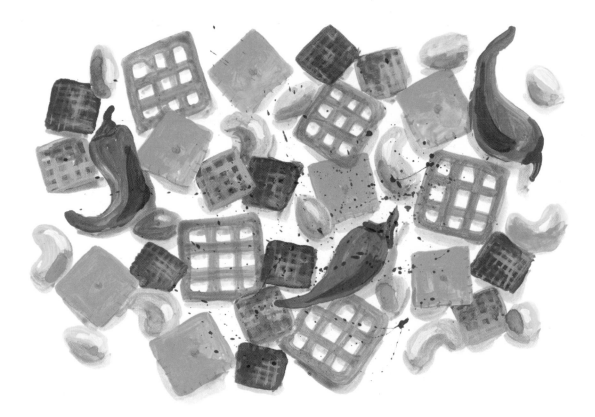

Tic-Tac-Toe

What was the first strategy game you remember learning? There's a decent chance it was good ol' Tic-Tac-Toe, a classic game that teaches children the basics of strategic gameplay. Eventually, most kids develop a sense of the best opening move—usually claiming the middle or one of the corner squares. And, in time, kids learn that the first player to move has a serious—actually, insurmountable—advantage.

Tic-Tac-Toe, descended from the ancient Roman game Three Men's Morris, is an example of a solved game, meaning that the outcome of the game can be predicted from any position with perfect play. Even chess is partially solved, with certain endgame positions having predetermined outcomes among strong players who know the patterns. Of course, Tic-Tac-Toe is much simpler, and older kids eventually learn that they can force a draw (and maybe even chance a win) by playing first.

Other completely solved games include Connect Four, Hex, and Guess Who?

Hot & Sweet Chex Mix

MAKES ABOUT 10 CUPS

3 cups Corn Chex

3 cups Rice Chex

1 cup Cheez-Its, broken up if necessary

1 cup pretzel sticks or waffle pretzels

1 cup salted peanuts

1 cup salted cashews

8 tablespoons (1 stick) unsalted butter

2 tablespoons Worcestershire sauce

1 tablespoon sriracha

1 tablespoon soy sauce

2 teaspoons light brown sugar

1 teaspoon garlic salt

> **MAKE AHEAD:**
> The mix will keep, covered in an airtight container, for up to 2 weeks.

Who doesn't have fond memories of homemade Chex Party Mix? This classic crunchy snack has been around for many years and it continues to be a party and holiday favorite. Here is an updated version that adds sriracha for heat and brown sugar for a touch of sweetness to its buttery coating. I don't use Wheat Chex in the recipe simply because it's not my favorite. But feel free to customize the mix with any of your preferred ingredients, such as different cereals or nuts, bagel chips, or Goldfish, to name a few. Just make sure the combination amounts to about 10 cups.

Preheat the oven to 250°F. Line two large rimmed baking sheets with parchment paper.

Put the cereal, Cheez-Its, pretzels, peanuts, and cashews in a large mixing bowl and gently toss together.

Melt the butter in a small saucepan over medium heat. Whisk in the Worcestershire sauce, sriracha, soy sauce, brown sugar, and garlic salt to combine. Pour the butter mixture over the cereal mixture and toss to coat well.

Pour and spread the mixture onto the baking sheets and bake, stirring every 15 minutes, until lightly browned, about 60 minutes. Cool on paper towels before serving.

½ cup margarine

2 tablespoons Worcestershire sauce

1¼ teaspoons seasoned salt

¼ teaspoon garlic salt

3 cups Wheat Chex cereal

2 cups Rice Chex cereal

1½ cups nuts (peanuts, pecans, or cashews, or any combination)

1½ cups small pretzel rods or pretzel sticks

MAKE AHEAD: The mix will keep, covered in an airtight container, for up to 1 week before serving.

The Original Chex Party Mix

This is the original version of Chex Party Mix and it is based on the recipe taken directly off the back of a 1950s Chex cereal box. It was a wildly popular snack that was served at holiday parties and game nights. The original recipe used margarine instead of butter, most likely because butter was twice as expensive as margarine in those days.

Preheat the oven to 275°F.

Melt the margarine in a shallow pan over low heat. Stir in the Worcestershire sauce, seasoned salt, and garlic salt.

Combine the Wheat Chex, Rice Chex, nuts, and pretzel rods in a large bowl and drizzle with the margarine mixture. Carefully mix with a wooden spoon to avoid breaking the pretzels and cereal squares. Coat all the pieces evenly with the seasoned butter mixture.

Place the mix in a shallow baking pan with sides. Bake for 40 minutes, stirring every 10 minutes or so to evenly toast the mixture.

Let cool for 15 minutes.

Panfried Chickpeas

When panfrying chickpeas, it is important that they are very dry. To dry them, simply let them sit on a baking sheet lined with paper towels overnight. They will then crisp up in hot olive oil very nicely.

Two 15-ounce cans chickpeas, drained and rinsed

¾ tablespoon ground coriander

½ tablespoon ground cumin

½ tablespoon hot paprika

¾ cup olive oil

Kosher salt and freshly ground black pepper

2 tablespoons lemon zest

MAKE AHEAD:
The fried chickpeas will keep, at room temperature, for up to 4 hours.

Spread the chickpeas on a baking sheet lined with paper towels to dry thoroughly (this can be done 1 day in advance).

Combine the coriander, cumin, and paprika in a small bowl and set aside.

Heat the oil in a large skillet over medium-high heat. When the oil bubbles around a chickpea, it is ready for frying.

Add the chickpeas to the skillet and sauté, stirring frequently, until they are golden and crispy, 10 to 15 minutes. Using a slotted spoon, transfer the chickpeas to paper towels to drain briefly. Season with salt and pepper.

Transfer the chickpeas to a large bowl. Sprinkle with the spice mixture and toss to coat completely. Sprinkle with lemon zest and serve.

Cacio e Pepe Popcorn

¼ cup canola oil or
grapeseed oil

½ cup popcorn kernels

3 tablespoons unsalted
butter, melted

¼ cup freshly grated
Parmigiano-Reggiano
cheese

½ teaspoon kosher salt

½ teaspoon garlic salt

Freshly ground black pepper

This popcorn preparation is based on a recipe for cacio e pepe, the delicious pasta dish that is made with just a few simple ingredients. It really brings a whole new level of flavor to plain popcorn.

Heat the oil in a large pan with a lid over medium heat. When the oil is hot, add the popcorn kernels and shake the pan, gently tossing the kernels until they are all coated with oil. Cover with a lid slightly ajar to allow the steam to escape.

Cook until the popping slows to several seconds between pops. Remove from the heat, allow a minute or two for any final pops, and then pour the popcorn into a large bowl.

Drizzle the melted butter over the popcorn and add the cheese, kosher salt, garlic salt, and a generous amount of pepper, tossing occasionally until the popcorn is evenly coated. Serve immediately.

The Royal Game of Ur

One of the oldest board games, perhaps the oldest, was the Royal Game of Ur, a two-player strategic racing game where players rolled four-sided dice and tried to move tokens around and off their side of the board. An ancient precursor to games like backgammon and ludo, the Royal Game of Ur was played in ancient Mesopotamia as early as 3000 BC. While the dice are four-sided, the number of spaces the player moves is determined by the vertices, two of which are painted white on each dice. That means, unlike in modern dice games, a player could roll a zero and lose a turn!

Popcorn at the Movies

Who doesn't love getting that familiar whiff of hot popcorn upon entering a movie theater? Popcorn and movies are a winning combination, but how did popcorn become the default snack to eat at the cinema?

Here's a little history: In the mid-1800s, popcorn was a popular snack food that was sold at carnivals, fairs, and on the street. Movie theaters began to appear in the early 1900s and owners wanted to re-create the opulence of traditional theaters with plush carpeting and seats—eating and drinking were definitely not allowed in them. In addition, early movies were silent ones and the audience had to be able to read the text on the screens. Therefore, in the early years of doing business, theaters were considered upscale and they catered to a well-educated, wealthy crowd.

When movies with sound appeared in 1927, they became accessible to the masses and people wanted to bring their own snacks into the theater with them. Savvy street vendors spotted an opportunity and started selling their popcorn outside of movie theaters. Eventually, theater owners caught on and began selling it themselves from popcorn machines stationed inside their theaters. It made sense; popcorn was cheap to produce on a large scale and no special skills were needed to make it. It was a win for the audience too. Popcorn has always been the ideal snack to savor while watching a movie—you can eat it with your hands and without distraction.

So that's the story of popcorn and movies. It's a simple, tasty snack that audiences enjoy and that theaters make a large profit from. These days, we simply can't imagine watching a film without buying popcorn to munch on. It's part of the movie experience.

1⅔ cups unbleached all-purpose flour

1¼ teaspoons dry mustard

¼ teaspoon cayenne pepper

¼ teaspoon paprika

Kosher salt and freshly ground black pepper

8 ounces (2 cups) coarsely grated extra-sharp Cheddar cheese

4 ounces (1 stick) unsalted butter, at room temperature

2 tablespoons water

MAKE AHEAD:
The cheese straws will keep, covered in an airtight container, for 1 week.

Cheese Straws

Cheese straws have been a Southern party staple for many generations. These delightful, airy bites have a bit of a kick and they go well with all types of wine and cocktails. They can be made up to a week ahead of time and actually taste better after a day or two. When making them or any other dish that uses grated cheese, be sure to freshly grate the cheese: preshredded tends to clump together.

Whisk the flour, mustard, cayenne pepper, and paprika together in a medium bowl. Season with salt and pepper and set aside.

Using an electric mixer, beat the cheese and butter on low speed until well blended. Gradually beat in the flour mixture until completely incorporated. Add the water and beat for 1 minute.

Turn out the dough onto a lightly floured surface and knead about 10 times. On a large sheet of floured wax paper, roll the dough into a 12-by-9-inch rectangle. Slide the dough onto a baking sheet and refrigerate until chilled, about 15 minutes.

Position an oven rack in the center of the oven and preheat the oven to 425°F.

Using a sharp knife, cut the dough in half crosswise, then cut it into 6-by-¼-inch strips. Transfer the strips to two baking sheets. Bake for 15 minutes, or until the cheese straws are golden brown and crisp. Let cool slightly, then transfer to a rack to cool completely.

1½ pounds mixed olives, drained and rinsed

2 lemons, thinly sliced

1 fennel bulb, trimmed and thinly sliced lengthwise

4 garlic cloves, thinly sliced

2 tablespoons black peppercorns

1 tablespoon fennel seeds

Extra virgin olive oil, to cover

MAKE AHEAD:
The olives will keep, covered in the refrigerator, for up to 1 month. Bring to room temperature before serving.

Lemon-Fennel Olives

Homemade marinated olives are always a delicious addition to the table. They're plump, juicy, and beautiful, and very easy to prepare. Simply choose from a range of mixed olives, layer with thin slices of lemon and fennel, and pour fruity olive oil over them.

Put a layer of olives in the bottom of a clean 1-pint glass jar. Add several slices each of the lemon, fennel, and garlic, and sprinkle with some of the peppercorns and fennel seeds. Continue layering until the jar is full. Cover the olives with olive oil and seal the jar tightly. Repeat this process with the second 1-pint jar.

Refrigerate the olives for 24 hours before serving (see Make Ahead).

Crokinole

Though little-known in the United States, the game of Crokinole is a popular pastime north of the border in Canada. Combining elements of carrom, air hockey, shuffleboard, and curling, Crokinole is a tabletop dexterity game where players sit around a circular wooden board and try to score by shooting small discs into scoring areas. The center of the board is the most valuable area, but it's guarded by pegs, requiring players to navigate around the obstacles. Additionally, players will try to knock each other's discs off the board, so you never want to leave yourself too open to attack.

The Crokinole World Championship has been held in Ontario, Canada, since 1999, with categories for adult and youth singles and doubles play. Though primarily a Canadian phenomenon, the World Championship has also attracted participants from the United States, Spain, Germany, Australia, and the UK.

Deviled Eggs with Bacon & Horseradish

6 large eggs

½ cup mayonnaise

1 tablespoon prepared horseradish

1 teaspoon Dijon mustard

½ teaspoon white wine vinegar

2 tablespoons minced fresh chives

Kosher salt and freshly ground black pepper

2 slices smoky bacon

1 teaspoon olive oil

MAKE AHEAD: The deviled eggs can be refrigerated for up to 3 hours. Garnish with the bacon before serving.

Deviled eggs are a classic party snack, and I'm always up for trying new variations. This version, laced with tangy horseradish and topped with smoky bacon, is a real winner.

Put the eggs in a single layer in a large pot and add cold water to cover them. Bring to a gentle boil over medium-high heat. Remove from the heat and cover tightly. Let the eggs stand, covered, for 10 minutes.

Drain and rinse the eggs under cold water. Pat the eggs dry and let cool completely.

Peel the eggs carefully and cut them in half lengthwise. Gently scoop the yolks into a medium bowl, being careful not to break the whites. Arrange the egg whites, cavity side up, on a platter and set aside.

Mash the yolks with a fork. Add the mayonnaise, horseradish, mustard, and vinegar. Stir in the chives and blend well. Season with salt and pepper.

Meanwhile, stack the bacon slices and cut them crosswise into four pieces. Put them in the freezer and chill until firm, about 15 minutes. Cut the cold bacon into ⅛-inch pieces. Heat the oil in a large skillet over medium heat, add the bacon and cook, stirring occasionally, until crispy. Drain on paper towels.

Using a small spoon or a piping bag, mound the filling into the cavities of the egg white halves. Garnish the eggs with the crumbled bacon and serve.

6 large eggs

½ cup mayonnaise

1 teaspoon Dijon mustard

½ teaspoon paprika

½ teaspoon white wine vinegar

3 tablespoons crumbled smoked trout, skin and bones removed (see Note)

2 tablespoons chopped fresh watercress

Kosher salt and freshly ground black pepper

Watercress sprigs, for garnish

MAKE AHEAD: The deviled eggs can be refrigerated for up to 3 hours. Garnish before serving.

Deviled Eggs with Smoked Trout & Watercress

Smoked trout and fresh watercress are excellent additions to the creamy filling in these deviled eggs. If you can't find smoked trout, any other smoked fish will work well.

Put the eggs in a single layer in a large pot and add cold water to cover them. Bring to a gentle boil over medium-high heat. Remove from the heat and cover tightly. Let the eggs stand, covered, for 10 minutes.

Drain and rinse the eggs under cold water. Pat the eggs dry and let cool completely.

Peel the eggs carefully and cut them in half lengthwise. Gently scoop the yolks into a medium bowl, being careful not to break the whites. Arrange the egg whites, cavity side up, on a platter and set aside.

Mash the yolks with a fork. Add the mayonnaise, mustard, paprika, and vinegar. Stir in the trout and watercress and blend well. Season with salt and pepper.

Using a small spoon or a piping bag, mound the filling into the cavities of the egg white halves. Garnish the eggs with watercress sprigs and serve.

Note: Smoked trout is available in fish markets and specialty shops where high-quality smoked fish is sold.

MAKES ABOUT 24
ROUNDS; SERVES 6 TO 8

8 ounces cream cheese, at
room temperature

¾ cup mayonnaise

2 tablespoons chopped fresh
chives

2 tablespoons chopped fresh
dill

2 tablespoons chopped fresh
flat-leaf parsley

1 teaspoon lemon zest

Kosher salt and freshly
ground black pepper

1 large or 2 medium
cucumbers, cut into ¼-inch
rounds

3 to 4 ounces smoked
salmon, cut into strips

Fresh lemon juice, for
serving

Dill sprigs, for garnish

Cucumber Rounds with Whipped Cream Cheese & Smoked Salmon

These crunchy bites of cucumbers topped with a dollop
of whipped cream cheese, smoked salmon, and dill make
a lovely snack. They taste as good as they look.

Put the cream cheese, mayonnaise, chives, dill, parsley,
and lemon zest in a food processor and blend until smooth
and creamy. Season with salt and pepper and blend again
(see Make Ahead).

To serve, spread the tops of the cucumber rounds generously with the cream cheese mixture, top with strips
of smoked salmon, drizzle with lemon juice, and garnish
with dill sprigs.

MAKE AHEAD:
The cream cheese
spread will keep,
covered in the
refrigerator, for up
to 2 days. Bring to
room temperature
before assembling
and serving.

1 pound white and red onions, thinly sliced

3 large shallots, thinly sliced

2 thyme sprigs

¼ cup olive oil

Kosher salt and freshly ground black pepper

½ cup white wine

1 tablespoon white wine vinegar

1 cup sour cream

¼ cup plain whole-milk Greek yogurt

¼ cup minced fresh chives

MAKE AHEAD:
The dip will keep, covered in the refrigerator, for up to 3 days before serving.

Roasted Onion & Shallot Dip

This is not your ordinary onion dip made with soup mix. It is a savory blend of slow-roasted onions, shallots and thyme, sour cream, and Greek yogurt. Served with potato chips, it makes a superb snack.

Preheat the oven to 425°F.

Arrange the onions, shallots, and thyme sprigs on a large rimmed baking sheet. Pour the olive oil all over, season with salt and pepper, and stir.

Roast the onion mixture, stirring and scraping occasionally, until it turns golden brown, 30 to 40 minutes. Remove from the oven and discard the thyme sprigs. Add the wine and the vinegar; stir to scrape up any browned bits from the bottom of the pan. Return the onion mixture to the oven and continue roasting, stirring occasionally, until deep golden brown, 10 to 15 minutes longer. Remove and let cool.

Transfer the onion mixture to a cutting board and mince. Transfer to a medium bowl, stir in the sour cream, yogurt, and chives. Taste and adjust the seasoning, adding more salt and pepper if necessary. Cover and refrigerate at least 1 hour before serving (see Make Ahead).

½ cup mayonnaise

½ cup sour cream

3 tablespoons buttermilk

2 tablespoons minced fresh chives

2 teaspoons minced fresh thyme

1 medium garlic clove, mashed into a paste

Kosher salt and freshly ground black pepper

MAKE AHEAD: The dip will keep, covered in the refrigerator, for up to 2 days.

Herbed Buttermilk Ranch Dip

Here's a quick and easy dip that has a fresh herby flavor. It's very good with chips, pretzels, and crudités.

Whisk together the mayonnaise, sour cream, buttermilk, chives, thyme, and garlic in a medium bowl until very smooth. Season with salt and pepper. Taste and adjust the seasoning, if necessary, and add more buttermilk if the dip seems too thin. Cover and refrigerate the dip for at least 2 hours before serving (see Make Ahead).

REMOULADE SAUCE

1 cup mayonnaise

3 tablespoons ketchup

2 teaspoons Dijon mustard

2 teaspoons prepared
   horseradish

1 teaspoon Worcestershire
   sauce

2 teaspoons drained capers,
   finely chopped

1½ teaspoons Old Bay
   Seasoning

1 teaspoon fresh lemon juice

Kosher salt and freshly
   ground black pepper

SHRIMP

1½ pounds large shrimp,
   cooked, peeled, and
   deveined, tails left on (see
   Make Ahead)

**ASSORTED FRESH
CRUDITÉS**

Asparagus spears and green
   beans, trimmed, steamed,
   and chilled

Sugar snap peas, trimmed

Persian cucumbers,
   quartered lengthwise

Radishes, halved if large

Fennel, thinly sliced

Endive leaves

Crudités & Shrimp with Remoulade Sauce

Zesty remoulade sauce is the perfect accompaniment to a platter of crudités and chilled shrimp. Choose from a wide variety of colorful vegetables that look fresh and enticing to create a beautiful, delicious spread.

Put the mayonnaise, ketchup, mustard, horseradish, Worcestershire sauce, capers, Old Bay Seasoning, and lemon juice in a medium bowl and whisk together until smooth. Season with salt and pepper. Cover and refrigerate the remoulade sauce for at least 1 hour before serving (see Make Ahead).

To serve, arrange the shrimp and vegetables and a bowl of remoulade sauce on a large platter.

> **MAKE AHEAD:**
> The remoulade sauce will keep, covered in the refrigerator, for up to 5 days. Taste and adjust the seasoning, if necessary, and stir well before serving. The cooked shrimp will keep, covered in the refrigerator, for up to 1 day before serving.

4 plum tomatoes (about 1 pound), seeded and chopped into ¼-inch pieces

3 small or 2 large ripe mangoes, peeled and diced

1 medium red onion, finely chopped

1 medium red bell pepper, stemmed, seeded, and cut into ¼-inch pieces

4 teaspoons minced garlic

1 teaspoon red pepper flakes

¼ cup chopped fresh cilantro leaves

¼ cup pineapple juice

¼ cup orange juice

2 tablespoons white vinegar

Juice of 1 lime

> **MAKE AHEAD:**
> The salsa will keep, covered in the refrigerator, for up to 3 days.

Tomato-Mango Salsa

The combination of fresh mangoes and fruit juices blended with savory tomatoes and onions creates a marvelous twist on everyday salsa. In addition to serving with chips and crudités, it's very good served as a condiment with grilled salmon, swordfish, and shrimp.

Combine the tomatoes, mangoes, onion, bell pepper, garlic, pepper flakes, and cilantro in a large nonreactive bowl and mix gently.

Whisk the pineapple juice, orange juice, vinegar, and lime juice together in a separate small bowl. Add to the tomato mixture and mix gently. Cover and refrigerate for at least 1 hour before serving (see Make Ahead).

4 ripe plum tomatoes, coarsely chopped

2 tablespoons olive oil

Kosher salt and freshly ground black pepper

2 scallions (white and green parts), trimmed and minced

½ cup chopped red onion

½ cup chopped red bell pepper

1 tablespoon fresh lime juice

1 teaspoon ground cumin

1 teaspoon chili powder

> **MAKE AHEAD:**
> The salsa will keep, covered in the refrigerator, for up to 1 day.

Roasted Plum Tomato Salsa

We all love salsa made with fresh, ripe tomatoes, but they can be hard to come by year-round. Oven-roasted plum tomatoes make a hearty, deep-flavored salsa that's just right to serve with tortilla chips or tacos or to spread on grilled bread for savory bruschetta.

Preheat the oven to 350°F.

Put the tomatoes, 1 tablespoon of the olive oil, and salt and pepper in a large roasting pan and toss together. Roast the tomatoes, stirring occasionally, until tender, about 45 minutes. Remove from the oven and let cool.

Meanwhile, put the remaining 1 tablespoon of olive oil, scallions, onion, bell pepper, lime juice, cumin, and chili powder in a medium bowl and toss together.

Transfer the tomatoes to a cutting board and chop them finely. Add the tomatoes and their juices to the onion and pepper mixture and toss well. Taste and adjust the seasoning, adding more salt and pepper if necessary. Serve chilled or at room temperature (see Make Ahead).

Seafood Guacamole

This is a rich and luscious version of guacamole with crabmeat and shrimp added. It should be made shortly before serving. Serve with tortilla chips.

SEAFOOD

4 ounces lump crabmeat, picked over for shells

4 ounces baby shrimp, cooked, peeled, and left whole, or larger shrimp, cooked, peeled, and cut into pieces

2 tablespoons chopped fresh cilantro

2 tablespoons finely chopped jalapeño pepper

1 tablespoon olive oil

Kosher salt and freshly ground pepper

GUACAMOLE

3 ripe avocados, halved, pitted, and coarsely chopped

2 tablespoons fresh lime juice

½ red onion, diced

½ ripe tomato, coarsely chopped

2 tablespoons chopped fresh cilantro

Pinch of ground cumin

Kosher salt

Dash of hot sauce

FOR THE SEAFOOD: Toss the crabmeat, shrimp, cilantro, jalapeño pepper, olive oil, salt and pepper together in a nonreactive mixing bowl. Let stand at room temperature for 30 minutes.

TO MAKE THE GUACAMOLE: Scoop the avocado into a medium bowl. Add the lime juice and mash lightly with a fork. Gently mix in the onion, tomato, cilantro, and cumin, and continue to mash. Season with the salt and hot sauce and mash again until well mixed but not too smooth.

Fold in the marinated seafood and gently mix to combine. Taste and adjust the seasoning, if necessary.

GINGER SHRIMP

½ cup thinly sliced fresh
  ginger

½ cup rice vinegar

¼ cup sugar

Pinch of red pepper flakes

2 pounds large shrimp,
  peeled and deveined, tails
  left on

4 ice cubes

DIPPING SAUCE

⅓ cup sweet Thai chili sauce

3 tablespoons fresh lime
  juice

2 tablespoons ketchup

1½ teaspoons fish sauce

Fresh lime wedges for
  serving

> **MAKE AHEAD:**
> The shrimp can
> be marinated
> overnight. The
> dipping sauce will
> keep, covered in the
> refrigerator, for up
> to 2 days. Stir well
> before serving.

Ginger Shrimp Cocktail with Thai Dipping Sauce

This crowd-pleasing recipe is a refreshing riff on shrimp cocktail. Here, the shrimp is marinated with rice vinegar and a generous amount of fresh ginger. It is served with sweet and sour dipping sauce that can be made well ahead of time.

TO MAKE THE SHRIMP: Put the ginger, vinegar, sugar, and pepper flakes in a small saucepan. Bring to a boil over high heat and cook, stirring to dissolve the sugar. Transfer to a large bowl and let cool.

Bring a large pot of salted water to a boil over high heat. Add the shrimp, reduce the heat, and cook until they turn pink and are slightly firm to the touch, about 3 minutes. Drain the shrimp and add them to the ginger mixture. Stir in the ice cubes and refrigerate for at least 4 hours or overnight. Drain the shrimp and pat dry. Discard the ginger.

TO MAKE THE DIPPING SAUCE: Mix the chili sauce, lime juice, ketchup, and fish sauce together in a small bowl. Cover and refrigerate for at least 1 hour (see Make Ahead).

Arrange the shrimp and lime wedges on a platter and serve with the dipping sauce.

3 pounds bone-in, skin-on
chicken breasts, halved

1 small onion, halved

1 stalk celery, halved

1 small carrot, halved

10 sprigs fresh flat-leaf
parsley

2 sprigs fresh thyme

4 cups chicken broth

2 cups water

1 stalk celery, diced

4 scallions (white and green
parts), trimmed and thinly
sliced

1½ teaspoons finely chopped
fresh dill

2 tablespoons chopped fresh
flat-leaf parsley, plus more
for garnish

½ cup mayonnaise

½ cup plain Greek yogurt

2 teaspoons fresh lemon
juice

1 teaspoon Dijon mustard

Kosher salt and freshly
ground black pepper

½ cup chopped walnuts

½ cup seedless red grapes,
halved

3 heads Belgian endive
separated into leaves

> **MAKE AHEAD:**
> The chicken salad
> will keep, covered in
> the refrigerator, for
> up to 1 day.

Endive Leaves with Chicken, Walnut & Grape Salad

Crispy leaves of endive filled with chicken salad are a perfect finger food. It's best to make the chicken salad a day ahead of time to give the flavors time to intensify.

Put the chicken, onion, halved celery pieces, carrot, parsley, and thyme in a large soup pot. Cover with the broth and 2 cups of water and bring just to a boil. Reduce the heat to medium-low and simmer, partially covered, for 30 minutes. Remove from the heat, uncover, and let the chicken cool in the cooking liquid for 30 minutes.

Using tongs, transfer the chicken to a cutting board and reserve the broth. Remove and discard the skin and bones from the chicken; chop the chicken into small pieces and transfer to a large bowl. Strain the broth and store, covered, in the refrigerator for up to 3 days or freeze for later use. Remove any fat from the surface of the broth before using.

Add the diced celery, scallions, dill, and parsley to the chicken.

Combine the mayonnaise, yogurt, lemon juice, and mustard in a medium bowl. Season with salt and pepper and mix well. Add the walnuts and grapes to the chicken mixture and stir well to combine.

Taste and adjust the seasoning, if necessary. Cover and refrigerate until well chilled, at least 4 hours or overnight (see Make Ahead).

Spoon the chicken salad into the endive leaves and arrange on a platter. Top with chopped parsley and serve at once.

CRUST

**1⅓ cups unbleached
all-purpose flour**

1 tablespoon sugar

¼ teaspoon salt

**8 tablespoons (1 stick) cold
unsalted butter, cut into
½-inch cubes**

2 to 3 tablespoons ice water

FILLING

2 large eggs

¼ cup whole milk

**¼ cup heavy cream (see
Note)**

**Kosher salt and freshly
ground black pepper**

¼ cup cubed ham

**¼ cup grated white Cheddar
cheese**

**¼ cup grated Parmesan
cheese**

¼ cup finely minced chives

**Nonstick spray, for greasing
the muffin pans**

Ham & Cheese Mini Quiches

These savory mini quiches are sure to impress your friends at the table. The filling is made with ham, cheese, and chives, but you can use a variety of other ingredients such as scallions, peppers, mushrooms, bacon, or chorizo. You will need a mini muffin pan to make these quiches.

TO MAKE THE DOUGH: Combine the flour, sugar, and salt in a food processor and pulse to blend. Scatter the butter over the flour and pulse 10 to 15 times, or until the mixture resembles coarse meal, with some pea-size lumps of butter. Add 2 tablespoons of ice water and pulse briefly to incorporate. If the dough doesn't hold together, add a bit more water.

Turn the dough onto a large sheet of plastic wrap and knead for about 2 minutes.. Shape the dough into a disk, wrap it in plastic wrap, and refrigerate for at least 1 hour before rolling it out (see Make Ahead).

TO MAKE THE FILLING: Put the eggs, milk, and cream in a measuring cup with a spout and whisk together until completely combined, about 1 minute. Cover and refrigerate the filling. Season with salt and pepper.

Preheat the oven to 375°F. Spray the muffin pans with cooking spray.

Put the dough onto a floured work surface and roll into a 12-inch circle. Using a 2½-inch cookie cutter, cut into 24 rounds, rerolling the dough scraps a few times. Be sure to work quickly, as the dough becomes much more delicate as it gets warmer. You'll get about 24 rounds per pie crust.

CONTINUED →

Press and fit the dough rounds into and up the sides of each muffin cup. Pour the chilled filling evenly into each unbaked crust. Add the ham and sprinkle with the cheeses and chives.

Bake the quiches until the centers are set and the edges are lightly browned, about 25 minutes. Let them cool for about 5 minutes before removing from the pan. Serve warm or at room temperature.

Note: You can also use 1 cup of half-and-half instead of the milk and cream combination in the filling.

½ small white onion, finely chopped

3 garlic cloves, minced

½ teaspoon crushed red pepper flakes

1 teaspoon minced rosemary

1 teaspoon dried thyme leaves, crumbled

¼ cup fresh lemon juice

¼ cup extra-virgin olive oil

2 pounds boneless, skinless chicken thighs, cut into 1½-inch pieces

Kosher salt and freshly ground black pepper

Grilled Lemon-Rosemary Chicken Skewers

Skewers served straight from the grill make wonderful appetizers, and these tender bites of lemon- and herb-marinated chicken on a stick make a delicious hors d'oeuvre.

In a large bowl, whisk together the onion, garlic, red pepper flakes, rosemary, thyme, lemon juice, and olive oil; set aside ¼ cup of the marinade. Season the chicken with salt and pepper and add it to the large bowl. Mix well, cover, and marinate for 30 minutes to 1 hour.

Soak 12 bamboo skewers in cold water for at least 30 minutes. Prepare a charcoal or gas grill for medium heat.

Remove the chicken from the marinade and thread three pieces of the chicken onto each skewer; discard the marinade. Oil the grate and grill the chicken over moderate heat, turning occasionally and basting with the reserved marinade, until golden and cooked through, 12 to 15 minutes. Cover with aluminum foil until ready to serve.

**MAKES ABOUT 48
PIECES; SERVES 6 TO 8**

1½ pounds kielbasa sausage

**2 teaspoons grated orange
zest**

**¾ cup dry red wine, such as
Côtes du Rhône**

Kielbasa Bites with Red Wine & Orange Zest

These savory little bites get a tart citrusy flavor from grated orange zest. They require almost no work and are always a hit with the crowd.

Preheat the oven to 400°F.

Slice the sausage on the diagonal about ½-inch thick. Spread the slices in a large baking dish and bake until lightly browned, about 15 minutes.

Turn the sausages, sprinkle the orange zest over them, and pour in the wine. Bake for 10 minutes longer. Serve them hot or at room temperature with toothpicks.

MOVIE NIGHT

It's always fun to have your friends over to settle in and watch a great movie together. Here is a very sophisticated menu that elevates everyday movie snacks and drinks to a whole new level of tastes.

Menu

SNACKS
- Cacio e Pepe Popcorn (page 22)
- Lemon-Fennel Olives (page 26)

MAINS
- Bruschetta with Warm Spinach & Chickpeas (page 101)
- Bruschetta with Roasted Bell Peppers, Mozzarella & Anchovies (page 102)
- Antipasto Platter (page 73)

DESSERT
- Olive Oil Cake with Lemon Crème Fraîche (page 125)

DRINKS
- Lucky Dog (page 150)
- Homemade Lemonade (page 166)

Game Plan

1 MONTH AHEAD
Prepare the olives.

1 DAY AHEAD
Bake the olive oil cake.

Prepare and refrigerate the lemon crème fraîche.

Prepare and refrigerate the lemonade.

DAY OF
Prepare and assemble the ingredients for bruschetta before grilling bread. The spinach and chickpeas can be made a few hours ahead of time and reheated before serving.

Prepare and assemble the antipasto platter up to 2 hours before serving.

Prepare the bar for drinks.

Make the popcorn and serve.

The 100 Greatest Movies of All Time

1. *Citizen Kane* (1941)
2. *Casablanca* (1942)
3. *The Godfather* (1972)
4. *Gone with the Wind* (1939)
5. *Lawrence of Arabia* (1962)
6. *The Wizard of Oz* (1939)
7. *The Graduate* (1967)
8. *On the Waterfront* (1954)
9. *Schindler's List* (1993)
10. *Singin' in the Rain* (1952)
11. *It's a Wonderful Life* (1946)
12. *Sunset Boulevard* (1950)
13. *The Bridge on the River Kwai* (1957)
14. *Some Like It Hot* (1959)
15. *Star Wars* (1977)
16. *All About Eve* (1950)
17. *The African Queen* (1951)
18. *Psycho* (1960)
19. *Chinatown* (1974)
20. *One Flew Over the Cuckoo's Nest* (1975)
21. *The Grapes of Wrath* (1940)
22. *2001: A Space Odyssey* (1968)
23. *The Maltese Falcon* (1941)
24. *Raging Bull* (1980)
25. *E.T.: The Extra-Terrestrial* (1982)
26. *Dr. Strangelove or: How I Learned to Stop Worrying and Love the Bomb* (1964)
27. *Bonnie and Clyde* (1967)
28. *Apocalypse Now* (1979)
29. *Mr. Smith Goes to Washington* (1939)
30. *The Treasure of the Sierra Madre* (1948)
31. *Annie Hall* (1977)
32. *The Godfather Part II* (1974)
33. *High Noon* (1952)
34. *To Kill a Mockingbird* (1962)
35. *It Happened One Night* (1934)
36. *Midnight Cowboy* (1969)
37. *The Best Years of Our Lives* (1946)
38. *Double Indemnity* (1944)
39. *Doctor Zhivago* (1965)
40. *North by Northwest* (1959)
41. *West Side Story* (1961)
42. *Rear Window* (1954)
43. *King Kong* (1933)
44. *The Birth of a Nation* (1915)
45. *A Streetcar Named Desire* (1951)
46. *A Clockwork Orange* (1971)
47. *Taxi Driver* (1976)

48. *Jaws* (1975)

49. *Snow White and the Seven Dwarfs* (1937)

50. *Butch Cassidy and the Sundance Kid* (1969)

51. *The Philadelphia Story* (1940)

52. *From Here to Eternity* (1953)

53. *Amadeus* (1984)

54. *All Quiet on the Western Front* (1930)

55. *The Sound of Music* (1965)

56. *M*A*S*H* (1970)

57. *The Third Man* (1950)

58. *Fantasia* (1942)

59. *Rebel Without a Cause* (1955)

60. *Raiders of the Lost Ark* (1981)

61. *Vertigo* (1958)

62. *Tootsie* (1982)

63. *Stagecoach* (1939)

64. *Close Encounters of the Third Kind* (1977)

65. *The Silence of the Lambs* (1991)

66. *Network* (1976)

67. *The Manchurian Candidate* (1962)

68. *An American in Paris* (1951)

69. *Shane* (1953)

70. *The French Connection* (1971)

71. *Forrest Gump* (1994)

72. *Ben-Hur* (1959)

73. *Wuthering Heights* (1939)

74. *The Gold Rush* (1925)

75. *Dances with Wolves* (1990)

76. *City Lights* (1931)

77. *American Graffiti* (1973)

78. *Rocky* (1976)

79. *The Deer Hunter* (1978)

80. *The Wild Bunch* (1969)

81. *Modern Times* (1936)

82. *Giant* (1956)

83. *Platoon* (1986)

84. *Fargo* (1996)

85. *Duck Soup* (1933)

86. *Mutiny on the Bounty* (1935)

87. *Frankenstein* (1931)

88. *Easy Rider* (1969)

89. *Patton* (1970)

90. *The Jazz Singer* (1928)

91. *My Fair Lady* (1964)

92. *A Place in the Sun* (1951)

93. *The Apartment* (1960)

94. *Goodfellas* (1990)

95. *Pulp Fiction* (1994)

96. *The Searchers* (1956)

97. *Bringing Up Baby* (1938)

98. *Unforgiven* (1992)

99. *Guess Who's Coming to Dinner?* (1967)

100. *Yankee Doodle Dandy* (1942)

CHAPTER 2
BIG PLATES & SIDES

Homemade Pizza Dough

MAKES TWO 12-INCH
PIZZAS

1 cup warm water

1 package active dry yeast

3 tablespoons olive oil, plus
more for brushing

Kosher salt

3 cups unbleached
all-purpose flour, plus
more for dusting

What is more scrumptious than homemade pizza fresh out of the oven? Pizza is great to serve at parties because it can be as simple or as elaborate as you wish. Pizza dough and sauce can be made from scratch, or you can buy premade dough and good-quality tomato sauce from the supermarket or any local gourmet market or pizzeria. I recommend investing in a pizza stone and paddle; they make a big difference in the authenticity of the crust and overall quality of the pizza. But in a pinch, sturdy baking sheets will do.

Pour the warm water into a large bowl. Sprinkle the yeast over it and let stand until the yeast dissolves and gets a little foamy, about 5 minutes. Whisk in the olive oil and a pinch of salt. Using a wooden spoon, beat in the flour, $\frac{1}{2}$ cup at a time, until a soft and sticky dough forms; you may not need all the flour. Turn out the dough onto a lightly floured work surface and knead until smooth, 8 to 10 minutes. Dust with flour as needed to prevent sticking.

Brush another large bowl with olive oil. Divide the dough into two balls and transfer to the bowl. Cover with a clean kitchen towel and let rise in a warm place until doubled in bulk, about $2\frac{1}{2}$ hours.

If using the dough right away, gently separate the balls of dough (if needed) and place on a lightly dusted work surface. When you flatten the balls, gently press out the air with the palm of your hand, and proceed with the recipe as directed.

If not using the dough right away, store it in the refrigerator for up to 1 day. Bring it to room temperature before rolling out. Or wrap the dough tightly and freeze it for up to 1 month. Thaw the dough in the refrigerator before using, about 3 hours. Bring it to room temperature before rolling out.

Using Store-Bought Pizza Dough

If you don't have time or choose not to make pizza dough from scratch, you can buy prepared dough from the supermarket. Pizza dough is remarkably forgiving when it comes to storing and traveling, and good-quality store-bought versions can usually be found in the dairy section in supermarkets. Other good sources include specialty Italian markets or your favorite pizza place. Pizza dough is a wonderful thing to have on hand in your refrigerator or freezer, as it's the foundation for making an easy and delicious meal.

Dough Tips:

- Allow refrigerated dough to come to room temperature before working with it.
- Roll out the dough as thinly as possible before adding toppings.
- If you're not using the dough right away (and it hasn't already been frozen), freeze it, wrapped tightly in plastic wrap, within 2 days of buying it. It will last for up to 1 month. Thaw it in the refrigerator for about 3 hours. Bring it up to room temperature before rolling it out.

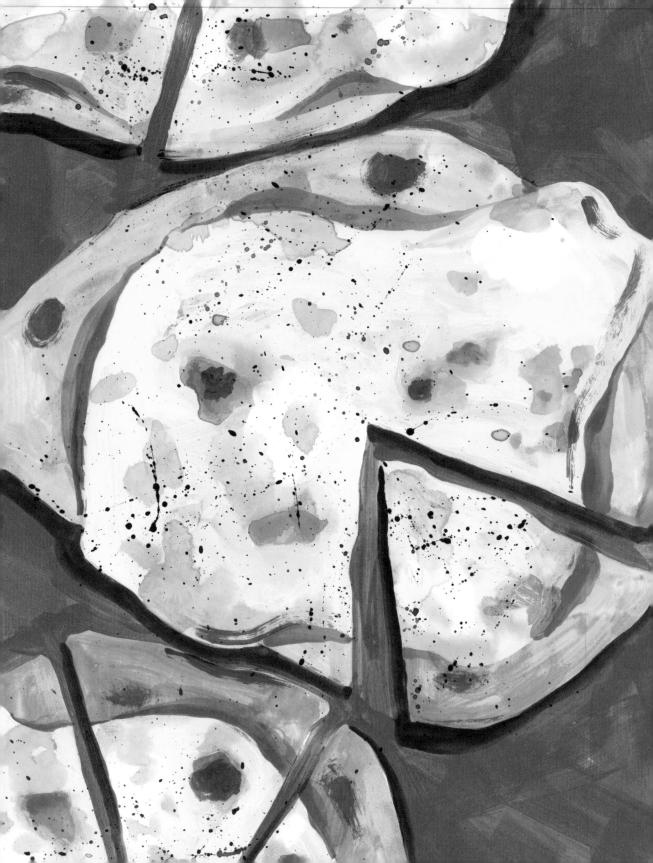

TOMATO SAUCE

1½ tablespoons olive oil

4 garlic cloves, thinly sliced

One 28-ounce can crushed
tomatoes, with their juices

Kosher salt and freshly
ground black pepper

½ cup chopped fresh basil
leaves

PIZZA

Pizza dough for 2 pizzas
(page 54)

Yellow cornmeal for dusting

2 cups (about ½ pound)
grated mozzarella cheese

1 cup (about ½ pound)
grated fontina cheese

½ cup freshly grated
Parmesan cheese

½ cup chopped fresh basil

Three-Cheese Pizza

There are so many varied and wonderful ingredients that you can add to homemade pizza, but you'll never go wrong making a classic pie topped with tomato sauce and cheese. Be sure to have all of your ingredients ready to go when prepping this because you need to work fast to get the pizzas in the oven.

TO MAKE THE TOMATO SAUCE: Heat the oil over medium heat in a large saucepan and sauté the garlic until golden, about 2 minutes. Do not let the garlic burn. Add the tomatoes, season with salt and pepper and simmer, uncovered, until the sauce is thickened, about 30 minutes. Add the basil and cook a few minutes more. Taste and adjust the seasoning, if necessary.

TO MAKE THE PIZZA: Preheat the oven to 450°F and put a pizza stone or heavy-bottomed baking sheet in it to heat.

Flatten half of the dough on a surface dusted with cornmeal. Using a rolling pin, roll out the dough to roughly 12 inches in diameter, about ½-inch thick. Dust a pizza paddle or baking sheet with cornmeal and transfer the pizza dough onto it. Working very quickly, spoon half of the sauce over the dough and spread evenly. Sprinkle half of the cheeses evenly over the sauce, and top with half of the basil. Slide the pizza onto the pizza stone or baking sheet and bake until the dough is golden brown and the cheese is bubbly and golden, 15 to 20 minutes. Repeat for the other pizza.

More Pizza Ideas

The fun part of making your own pizza is experimenting with the many variations and combinations of ingredients for toppings. It just depends on your taste and what you have on hand.

Here are a few scrumptious pizza combos to try:
- Caramelized leeks, goat cheese, and sweet Italian sausage
- Caramelized red onions and gorgonzola cheese
- Slow-cooked tomatoes, Taleggio cheese, and sautéed wild mushrooms
- Slow-cooked onions and roasted peppers, mozzarella cheese, and pancetta
- Sautéed Swiss chard, prosciutto, and Parmesan cheese
- Sautéed bell peppers, mozzarella cheese, and hot Italian sausage
- Sautéed spinach, mozzarella cheese, and prosciutto

Blackjack

It's been often claimed that Blackjack is the best game to play at a casino to win money (or perhaps, lose the least money). This sentiment is rooted in some truth. Blackjack is of course heavily influenced by random chance, but the odds of the game are calculable, with players able to follow some basic rules in order to maximize their chances of winning a hand.

Players can memorize what are called hit tables, essentially a chart that tells you whether to hit, stand, or double-down based on both your card and the dealer's. For example, probability says that you should stand on a 16 when the dealer has a 6 or under for his or her upcard, but hit if the dealer shows a 7 through ace. If you can commit to memory all 200 recommended moves for all the different possible positions, you can always play optimally. That might suck some fun out of the game, but it could pay off big!

Who Invented Monopoly?

Monopoly has been around for a long time and it has a remarkable history that dates back to the early 20th century.

Most people think that the game was invented by a man named Charles Darrow during the Great Depression and that he sold it to Parker Brothers for a large sum of money.

The true story is that the game was invented by a woman, Elizabeth Magie, as a protest against the big money of the Gilded Age. At that time the amount of wealth that was created in this country was in the hands of very few families, such as the Carnegies, Rockefellers, and Vanderbilts. Magie created a board game called The Landlord's Game to teach and raise awareness about the evils of business monopolies. She patented it in 1904 and the game became very popular.

Over thirty years later, at the height of the Great Depression, an unemployed Philadelphia man named Charles Darrow discovered the game, made his own version, and sold the rights to Parker Brothers in 1935.

Hasbro acquired Parker Brothers in 1991 and they acknowledge that Monopoly was inspired by Magie, who died in 1948. But her story has long been overshadowed by Darrow's rags to riches tale and he got all the credit for inventing the game.

No matter whose story is to be believed, the popularity of Monopoly lives on. Today the game is played in over 115 countries in 45 different languages.

MAKES 16 TACOS;
SERVES 8

CILANTRO-LIME SAUCE

3 tablespoons fresh lime juice

2 garlic cloves, minced

½ cup chopped fresh cilantro

½ jalapeño pepper, seeded and chopped

½ cup mayonnaise

½ cup sour cream

Pinch of sugar

Kosher salt and freshly ground black pepper

SHRIMP TACOS

3 tablespoons adobo (from 1 can chiles in adobo)

2 tablespoons honey

2 pounds medium shrimp, peeled and deveined

Kosher salt

16 corn or flour tortillas

4 tablespoons vegetable oil

2 small red onions, thinly sliced

½ head of green cabbage, thinly sliced

Hot sauce for serving
Lime wedges for serving

MAKE AHEAD: The cilantro-lime sauce will keep, covered in the refrigerator, for up to 1 day.

Shrimp Tacos with Cilantro-Lime Sauce

Cilantro-lime sauce and shrimp are a perfect combination of tastes in these luscious, elegant tacos. When serving these, be sure that all the garnishes are ready to go since the shrimp take only a few minutes to cook.

TO MAKE THE SAUCE: Put the lime juice, garlic, cilantro, jalapeño, and mayonnaise in a food processor and blend until smooth. Add the sour cream and sugar, season with salt and pepper and blend again to combine. Transfer to a bowl and set aside (see Make Ahead).

TO MAKE THE TACOS: Whisk together the adobo and honey in a large bowl to combine. Add the shrimp, season with salt, and toss to coat. Set aside and let marinate for 30 minutes.

Preheat the oven to 350°F. Put the tortillas on baking sheets and heat until warmed through, 3 to 5 minutes. Transfer the tortillas to a platter.

Heat half of the oil in a large skillet over medium-high heat. Add half of the shrimp mixture and cook, turning once, until bright pink and cooked through, 3 to 5 minutes. Transfer to a platter. Repeat with the remaining oil and shrimp and transfer to a platter.

Spoon the shrimp, onions, cabbage, and sauce into the tortillas. Serve with hot sauce and lime wedges.

MAKE AHEAD:
The barbecued turkey will keep, covered in the refrigerator, for up to 2 days. Bring to room temperature before reheating.

TURKEY

2 tablespoons olive oil

½ medium red onion, finely
chopped

2 garlic cloves, thinly sliced

1 jalapeño pepper, stemmed,
seeded, and finely chopped

½ teaspoon ground cumin

½ teaspoon Mexican
oregano

4 cups cooked shredded
turkey

¾ cup dark Mexican beer,
such as Modelo

½ cup barbecue
sauce, homemade or
store-bought

¼ cup apple cider vinegar

Kosher salt and freshly
ground black pepper

Hot sauce (optional), plus
more for serving

CABBAGE SLAW

¼ cup apple cider vinegar

2 teaspoons sugar

Kosher salt and freshly
ground black pepper

4 cups thinly sliced green
cabbage

16 corn or flour tortillas

Sliced avocados, sour cream,
chopped fresh cilantro, and
lime wedges for garnish

Barbecued Turkey Tacos

Turkey tacos are the perfect dish to serve to a crowd,
and they're especially good to make if you have leftovers
from the holiday bird and can't face yet another turkey
sandwich. Barbecued turkey is very easy to prepare and
tastes great tucked into tacos with a simple slaw and lots
of condiments.

TO MAKE THE TURKEY: Heat the oil in a large pot or
Dutch oven over medium heat. Add the onion, garlic, jalapeño pepper, cumin, and oregano and cook, stirring, until
the onion is softened, 5 to 8 minutes. Add the turkey and
cook, stirring, until evenly coated.

Add the beer, barbecue sauce, and vinegar, stir well, and
bring to a simmer. Season with salt and pepper, and add
hot sauce, if using. Simmer over low heat, stirring occasionally, for about 25 minutes (see Make Ahead).

TO MAKE THE CABBAGE SLAW: Combine the vinegar
and sugar in a small saucepan and season with salt and
pepper. Cook over medium heat until the sugar dissolves.

Put the cabbage in a large bowl, pour the hot vinegar mixture over it, toss to combine, and set aside.

Preheat the oven to 350°F. Put the tortillas on baking
sheets and heat until warmed through, 3 to 5 minutes.
Transfer the tortillas to a platter.

Spoon the turkey filling and cabbage slaw into the tortillas. Serve with avocado, sour cream, cilantro, lime
wedges, and additional hot sauce.

3 tablespoons olive oil

1 red onion, finely diced

3 garlic cloves, minced

1 red bell pepper, stemmed, seeded, and finely chopped

2 jalapeño peppers, stemmed, seeded, and finely chopped

2 teaspoons ground cumin

2 teaspoons chili powder

Two 15-ounce cans black beans, drained and rinsed

1 cup chopped fresh or canned tomatoes, with their juice

Kosher salt and freshly ground black pepper

4 cups chopped fresh baby spinach

16 corn or flour tortillas

¾ cup shredded Monterey Jack cheese

Sliced avocados, chopped fresh tomatoes, chopped fresh cilantro, lime wedges, and hot sauce for garnish

MAKE AHEAD:
The bean and spinach mixture can be cooked a few hours ahead of time and refrigerated. Bring to room temperature before reheating.

Black Bean & Spinach Tacos

These hearty and delicious tacos, made with black beans and spinach, will please vegetarians and meat eaters alike. You can assemble them yourself or, better yet, put all the garnishes out so that your guests can assemble and customize their own tacos.

Heat 2 tablespoons of the olive oil in a large skillet over medium heat. Add the onion, garlic, red pepper, and jalapeño peppers and cook until softened, about 5 minutes. Add the cumin and chili powder and cook, stirring occasionally, for 3 minutes.

Add the beans and tomatoes, season with salt and pepper, and cook over medium heat, stirring occasionally, until the liquid is absorbed, about 15 minutes.

Meanwhile, heat the remaining tablespoon of oil in a skillet. Add the spinach and sauté until just wilted, about 3 minutes. Set aside. Add the spinach to the beans and cook, stirring, until combined (see Make Ahead).

Preheat the oven to 350°F. Put the tortillas on baking sheets and heat until warmed through, 3 to 5 minutes. Transfer the tortillas to a large platter.

Spoon the bean mixture into the tortillas and sprinkle with the shredded cheese. Serve with avocados, tomatoes, cilantro, lime wedges, and hot sauce.

The Seventh-Inning Stretch

The seventh-inning stretch is a longtime baseball tradition. The origins of this ritual are unclear but there are a few theories about it. One popular one is that in 1910 William Howard Taft, America's 27th president, attended the opening-day game of the Washington Senators at Griffith Stadium and threw out the ceremonial first pitch (inaugurating the custom of the first pitch of the season being tossed out by the commander in chief). As the story goes, by the seventh inning the president, who was a very large man, was feeling cramped in his seat and got up to stretch his legs. The respectful crowd, thinking the president was leaving the stadium, rose to its feet—and supposedly the stretch was born.

Another theory states that a man called Brother Jasper of Mary, the baseball coach at New York City's Manhattan College, invented the ritual when he asked for a timeout in the middle of the seventh inning during a long game on a hot day in 1882. He saw that the fans were getting antsy and told them to stand up and stretch. Brother Jasper repeated this practice at following games, and the ritual moved to the major leagues when Manhattan College played exhibition games against the New York Giants in the late 1880s.

No matter how this custom came to be, music eventually became part of the seventh-inning stretch. In 1976, Harry Caray, the announcer for the Chicago White Sox, popularized the singing of "Take Me Out to the Ball Game." Today this iconic tune is played and sung during the seventh-inning stretch at many major-league ballparks across the country.

Horseshoes

While folks originally passed the time by hurling real horseshoes at a stake, it wasn't long until players started to fashion more standardized equipment specifically for gameplay. Actual horseshoes are small and nearly circular, with only a narrow opening. Modern horseshoes developed for the game are much wider and U-shaped, allowing for that classic, satisfying ringer.

Perhaps the most famous horseshoe pit is the one at the White House in Washington, D.C. Located on the South Lawn, it was established by Harry S. Truman. President George H. W. Bush was a skilled and passionate player of the game, and made the most use out of the pit after having it renovated. When Queen Elizabeth II visited the White House in 1991, she gifted the president a pair of silver-plated horseshoes. Those probably aren't regulation, but they sure are nice!

2 tablespoons minced garlic

2 tablespoons minced ginger

¼ cup gochujang (Korean chili paste)

½ cup soy sauce

2 tablespoons rice vinegar

2 teaspoons honey

3 pounds chicken wings: drumettes and wingettes

Chopped fresh cilantro for garnish

Minced scallions for garnish

Gochujang Chicken Wings

Gochujang is a red chili paste that is a mainstay ingredient in Korean cooking. It is quite thick and sticky and has a deep and pungent flavor. Here it is used in a marinade for chicken wings, and it gives them a good hot and spicy kick. Gochujang can be found in Asian markets and online.

Whisk the garlic, ginger, gochujang, soy sauce, vinegar, and honey together in a large nonreactive bowl. Add the chicken drumettes and wingettes and toss to coat evenly. Cover and let marinate in the refrigerator at least 2 hours or overnight.

Preheat the oven to 375°F.

Line two large rimmed baking sheets with aluminum foil. Remove the chicken pieces from the bowl and reserve the marinade. Arrange them on the baking sheets.

Bake the chicken for 10 minutes on each side, brushing occasionally with the remaining marinade. Flip once more and bake for 5 minutes. Remove from the oven and transfer to a large platter. Garnish with cilantro and scallions and serve immediately.

Pulled Pork Sliders

When making these very tasty sliders, be sure to give yourself enough time to prep them. The pork should marinate in the dry rub—overnight is best—and then cook slowly in the oven on low heat. For the barbecue sauce, you can make your own or use your favorite store-bought brand. These sliders taste terrific topped with Cabbage & Fennel Coleslaw (page 79).

PULLED PORK

1 pork roast (3 to 4 pounds), preferably pork shoulder or Boston butt

1 tablespoon olive oil

DRY RUB

3 tablespoons paprika

1 tablespoon kosher salt

1 tablespoon granulated sugar

1 tablespoon brown sugar

1 tablespoon ground cumin

1 tablespoon chili powder

1 teaspoon cayenne pepper

Freshly ground black pepper

BARBECUE SAUCE

1 tablespoon corn oil

1 small yellow onion, finely chopped

2 garlic cloves, thinly sliced

1½ cups ketchup

¾ cup cider vinegar

½ cup firmly packed brown sugar

2 tablespoons chili powder

1 tablespoon Dijon mustard

Dash of hot sauce

16 slider (mini hamburger) rolls or 8 regular hamburger rolls, split

Pat the pork dry and brush with the olive oil.

TO MAKE THE DRY RUB: In a small bowl, stir together the paprika, salt, both sugars, cumin, chili powder, cayenne, and black pepper to taste. Rub the dry rub all over the pork, wrap in plastic wrap, and let marinate in the refrigerator for at least 4 hours or up to overnight.

Preheat the oven to 300°F. Put the pork on a rack in a large roasting pan and roast until an instant-read thermometer registers 170°F, 5 to 6 hours.

TO MAKE THE BARBECUE SAUCE: Heat the corn oil in a saucepan over medium heat. Add the onion and garlic and sauté until softened and golden, about 5 minutes. Add the ketchup, vinegar, brown sugar, chili powder, mustard, and hot sauce and stir to mix well. Simmer gently, stirring occasionally, until the sauce thickens and the flavors blend, 20 to 25 minutes. Taste and adjust the seasoning, if necessary.

Remove the pork roast from the oven and transfer to a cutting board or large platter. Tent loosely with aluminum foil and let rest for 15 to 20 minutes. "Pull" the pork apart with two forks to form shreds and transfer to a large bowl. Add the sauce to the shredded pork.

Spoon the pulled pork onto the bottom halves of the rolls, dividing it evenly. Replace the tops of the rolls; if using regular hamburger rolls, cut each sandwich in half. Serve at once.

Frittatas

Frittatas are very versatile and so easy to make. They can be served for breakfast, lunch, or dinner and eaten warm, cold, or at room temperature—and you can add all types of vegetables and meat to this savory egg dish. The general ratio for making a frittata is 8 eggs, ⅓ cup heavy cream or whole milk, and ¾ cup of cheese. There are no hard and fast rules on what ingredients to add in, just make sure they are precooked.

Here are two simple frittata recipes that would be great to serve on a weekend when friends drop in to watch a game or a movie or to play cards.

8 eggs, at room temperature

⅓ cup heavy cream or whole milk

½ cup grated fontina cheese

¼ cup grated Parmesan cheese

Kosher salt and freshly ground black pepper

3 tablespoons olive oil

½ cup diced white or yellow onions

2 cups baby spinach

8 ounces Italian sausage, cooked, drained, and crumbled

SPINACH, SAUSAGE & CHEESE FRITTATA

Position an oven rack in the center of the oven and preheat the oven to 375°F.

Whisk together the eggs, cream, and cheeses in a medium bowl. Season with salt and pepper.

Heat the oil in a large skillet, preferably cast iron, over medium heat. Swirl the pan to coat the sides. Add the onions and cook until soft, about 5 minutes. Add the spinach and cook until wilted, about 2 minutes. Stir in the cooked sausage and spread evenly in the pan.

Pour the egg mixture over the spinach mixture and cook just until the edges start to pull away from the pan, 3 to 5 minutes. Transfer the skillet to the oven and bake until set, 16 to 18 minutes. Let it cool a bit and serve (see Make Ahead).

8 eggs, at room temperature

⅓ cup heavy cream or whole milk

½ cup grated Gruyère cheese

½ cup grated Parmesan cheese

Kosher salt and freshly ground black pepper

2 tablespoons olive oil

1 tablespoon unsalted butter

½ cup diced red onion

½ cup diced and seeded red bell pepper

½ cup diced zucchini

¼ cup minced scallions (white and green parts)

MAKE AHEAD: Once the frittata is cooled to room temperature, it can stand for up to an hour. It can also be covered and refrigerated up to 1 day. Serve cold, bring to room temperature, or reheat before serving.

VEGETABLE & CHEESE FRITTATA

Position an oven rack in the center of the oven and pre-heat the oven to 375°F.

Whisk together the eggs, cream, Gruyère cheese, and ¼ cup of the Parmesan cheese in a medium bowl. Season with salt and pepper.

Heat the oil and butter in a large skillet, preferably cast iron, over medium heat. Swirl the pan to coat the sides. Add the onions, peppers, zucchini, and scallions and cook until soft, 5 to 7 minutes.

Pour the egg mixture over the vegetable mixture and cook just until the edges start to pull away from the pan, 3 to 5 minutes. Transfer the skillet to the oven and bake. After 8 minutes, sprinkle the top of the frittata with the remaining Parmesan cheese. Continue baking until set, about 10 minutes. Let cool a bit and serve (see Make Ahead).

CHIMICHURRI SAUCE

½ cup chopped fresh
  flat-leaf parsley

¼ cup chopped fresh cilantro

4 large garlic cloves, minced

3 tablespoons red wine
  vinegar

1 tablespoon crushed fresh
  oregano leaves

1 teaspoon red pepper flakes

Kosher salt and freshly
  ground pepper

½ cup extra-virgin olive oil

MEATBALLS

1 garlic clove, grated

2 tablespoons drained
  capers, finely chopped

¼ cup chopped walnuts

1 large egg, beaten

1 tablespoon paprika

3 tablespoons extra-virgin
  olive oil

1 cup panko (Japanese
  breadcrumbs)

1½ pounds ground beef
  (20% fat)

Kosher salt and freshly
  ground black pepper

MAKE AHEAD:
The sauce will keep,
covered in the
refrigerator, for up to
3 days. Bring to room
temperature and stir
before serving.

Meatballs & Chimichurri Sauce

Meatballs are great party food and they're especially good to serve with chimichurri sauce, a garlicky green sauce that's made with fresh herbs, vinegar, and olive oil. This excellent condiment also pairs beautifully with grilled meat and fish, and it can be made well ahead of time.

TO MAKE THE CHIMICHURRI SAUCE: Put the parsley, cilantro, garlic, vinegar, oregano, and red pepper flakes in a food processor and blend until smooth. Season with salt and pepper. Transfer the sauce to a bowl, pour ½ cup olive oil over the mixture, and gently stir. Let the sauce stand for at least 20 minutes before serving (see Make Ahead).

TO MAKE THE MEATBALLS: Position an oven rack in the center of the oven and preheat the oven to 425°F.

Put the garlic, capers, and walnuts in a large bowl. Whisk in the egg, paprika, 1 tablespoon of the oil, and panko and combine.

Using clean hands, add the beef and mix gently with your hands until incorporated, but do not overmix. Season with salt and pepper and mix again. At this point, you can pinch off a little piece of the meatball mixture, sauté it in a skillet with a bit of oil, and taste and adjust the seasoning, if necessary.

Drizzle the remaining 2 tablespoons of oil on a rimmed baking sheet. Roll the beef mixture into 1-inch balls and arrange them on the pan.

Bake the meatballs, shaking the pan halfway through, until crispy on all sides, about 10 minutes.

Transfer the meatballs to a platter and serve with the chimichurri sauce with small forks or toothpicks.

Antipasto

Antipasto literally means "before the meal" in Italian. A traditional anti-pasto platter is made up of a variety of cured meats, cheeses, and raw, cooked, pickled, or marinated vegetables. Other accoutrements such as breads, toasts, and bread sticks are also an integral part of the platter.

For busy game night hosts who don't have the time to cook, or who prefer not to, an antipasto platter is the perfect thing to serve your guests. All it takes is a bit of planning ahead and some smart shopping. Look for the ingredients to prepare a sumptuous platter at gourmet shops, delicatessens, and local Italian and other ethnic shops. Excellent ingredients can also be ordered online.

MEATS: Serve a variety of cured meats such as prosciutto, soppressata, bresaola, salami, capicola, pepperoni, and mortadella. A word here about *salumi:* Although it is often confused with salami, *salumi* is simply a term for Italian-cured or preserved meat, mostly pork-based. *Salumi* meats are salt-cured, smoked, and fermented and some, such as sausages and pâtés, are preserved in fat.

CHEESES: Tasty, well-chosen cheeses are essential to an antipasto plat-ter, and they taste wonderful with salty meats, olives, and drinks. Be sure to serve a wide range of cheeses that vary in size, shape, texture, and fla-vor profiles.

SEAFOOD: You may want to serve some seafood along with the meat, cheese, and vegetables on the antipasto platter. Look for good-quality canned tuna and anchovies, and cooked and chilled squid, baby clams, and shrimp in the seafood section of the market or fish store. If you're up for cooking, prepare some clams or mussels on the half shell. These sea-food bites are excellent additions to an antipasto platter.

CONTINUED →

VEGETABLES: Serve a wide range of raw and cooked vegetables to add color, texture, and crunch to the platter. Red and yellow bell peppers, cherry tomatoes, slices of fresh fennel, celery sticks, and cucumber rounds drizzled with extra-virgin olive oil and sprinkled with sea salt and fresh herbs will look and taste terrific. Pickled and marinated vegetables, such as artichokes, cauliflower, mushrooms, pepperoncini, and roasted red peppers are readily available at the market. Other good fresh vegetables to cook and serve are steamed asparagus spears, cauliflower, and green beans, and roasted or grilled eggplant and zucchini.

BREADS: Good bread choices are baguettes and breadsticks, focaccia, ciabatta, and Cheese Straws (page 25). You may want to grill or toast small rounds of baguettes to make crostini.

MORE ACCENTS: Any number of tasty and beautiful accoutrements can be added to the platter. Good accompaniments include assorted nuts; dried fruit; jams, preserves, and chutneys; assorted mustards; olives and pickles; and very fresh fruit, such as apples, grapes, cherries, melon, and berries.

Given the wide range of choices of high-quality products that are on the market nowadays, it's very easy and fun to prepare and present a gorgeous and delicious antipasto platter that your guests will enjoy feasting on.

6 medium sweet potatoes, halved and cut into 3-inch wedges

2 tablespoons olive oil

½ teaspoon hot smoked paprika

½ teaspoon ground cinnamon

1 tablespoon crumbled fresh thyme leaves

Kosher salt

2 teaspoons lime zest

Roasted Sweet Potato Fries

Here is a very tasty and healthy alternative to french fries to serve alongside Pulled Pork Sliders (page 68). Paprika and cinnamon add a subtle smoky-sweet flavor to the fries, and they're finished with a sprinkle of lime zest. These fries are also a good accompaniment to grilled pork chops or roast chicken.

Preheat the oven to 350°F.

Put the sweet potatoes in a large bowl. Add the olive oil, paprika, and cinnamon and gently toss together to coat evenly. Spread the sweet potatoes on a baking sheet and sprinkle them with the thyme. Season with salt. Roast the potatoes in the oven until just crisp, about 1½ hours. Sprinkle with the lime zest and additional salt, if desired. Let the fries cool a bit before serving.

WILD RICE

1⅔ cups wild rice or wild rice blend, rinsed and drained

4 cups water or stock (or a combination)

Kosher salt

SALAD ASSEMBLY

½ cup diced celery

½ cup minced scallions (white and green parts)

½ cup dried cranberries

¼ cup pomegranate seeds, plus more for garnish

½ cup pecan halves, toasted and chopped

1 cup arugula

½ cup crumbled feta cheese

VINAIGRETTE

2 tablespoons white wine vinegar

¼ cup extra-virgin olive oil

½ garlic clove, minced

1 teaspoon sugar

Kosher salt and freshly ground black pepper

> **MAKE AHEAD:** The salad will keep, covered in the refrigerator, for up to 2 days. Bring to room temperature before garnishing and serving.

Wild Rice Salad

This salad is packed with great flavors that include chewy, nutty wild rice, peppery arugula, crunchy toasted pecans, and creamy feta cheese. Be sure to add some pomegranate seeds to the mix. Although they are a bit extravagant, they add a beautiful pop of color and sweetness to this earthy salad.

TO MAKE THE RICE: Put the rice in a large saucepan and add the water and salt. Bring to a boil over high heat. Reduce the heat to a simmer, cover and cook until the rice is chewy and some of the grains have burst open, about 45 minutes. Transfer the rice to a colander, drain, and let cool.

TO ASSEMBLE THE SALAD: Transfer the rice to a large bowl. There should be about 5 cups of cooked rice. Add the celery, scallions, cranberries, pomegranate seeds, and pecans and toss together.

TO MAKE THE VINAIGRETTE: Whisk the vinegar, olive oil, garlic, and sugar together until well combined. Season with salt and pepper. Pour the vinaigrette over the rice mixture and toss again (see Make Ahead).

TO SERVE: Just before serving, add the arugula to the salad and toss. Taste and adjust the seasoning, if necessary. Transfer the salad to a large serving bowl or platter. Sprinkle with feta cheese and pomegranate seeds.

½ head green cabbage, quartered, cored, and shredded

½ head red cabbage, quartered, cored, and shredded

1 fennel bulb, trimmed and very thinly sliced

2 carrots, peeled and finely shredded

6 scallions (white and green parts), finely minced

½ cup chopped fresh flat-leaf parsley

1½ cups mayonnaise

1½ cups plain low-fat yogurt

¼ cup packed light brown sugar

2 tablespoons prepared horseradish

2 tablespoons apple cider vinegar

Kosher salt and freshly ground black pepper

Cabbage & Fennel Coleslaw

This tangy version of slaw is made with apple cider vinegar and horseradish. It's a delicious addition to Pulled Pork Sliders (page 68), and it's a good dish to bring to a potluck party or picnic.

Put the cabbage, fennel, carrots, scallions, and parsley in a large bowl and toss to combine.

In a medium bowl, whisk the mayonnaise, yogurt, brown sugar, horseradish, and vinegar until well combined. Season with salt and pepper, taste and adjust the seasoning, if necessary, and whisk again.

Drizzle the dressing over the cabbage mixture and toss thoroughly. Cover and refrigerate the slaw for up to 6 hours before serving.

RICOTTA-PESTO SAUCE

¾ cup firmly packed fresh basil leaves

1 clove garlic, coarsely chopped

¼ cup pine nuts

½ cup extra-virgin olive oil

Pinch of salt

⅓ cup ricotta cheese

½ cup mascarpone cheese

GRILLED VEGETABLES

3 zucchinis, cut lengthwise into 1-inch-thick pieces

3 fennel bulbs, trimmed and cut lengthwise into ¼-inch-thick slices

2 red bell peppers, seeded, deveined, and cut into ½-inch-wide strips

2 yellow bell peppers, seeded, deveined, and cut into ½-inch-wide strips

¼ cup extra-virgin olive oil

Salt and freshly ground black pepper

> **MAKE AHEAD:**
> The sauce can be made up to 3 hours ahead of time and refrigerated. Bring to room temperature and stir well before serving.

Grilled Vegetables with Ricotta-Pesto Sauce

A platter heaped with colorful grilled vegetables surrounding a bowl of savory ricotta-pesto sauce makes a stunning presentation. Make this tasty summertime dish when basil is in season and plentiful.

TO MAKE THE SAUCE: Put the basil, garlic, pine nuts, olive oil, and salt in a food processor. Blend until smooth, scraping down the sides of the bowl as needed. Add the cheeses and pulse just until combined (see Make Ahead).

Prepare a charcoal or gas grill. Brush the grill rack lightly with oil or spray with vegetable oil spray to prevent sticking. If using charcoal, let the coals burn until medium-hot to hot.

Brush the vegetables generously with olive oil and season with salt and pepper. Arrange the zucchini and fennel on the grill rack and grill for about 4 minutes. Turn and grill for about 4 minutes longer, until lightly charred and tender. Grill the peppers for about 2 minutes and turn and grill for about 2 minutes longer, until lightly charred and tender.

Spoon the sauce into a bowl and set it in the center of a large platter. Arrange the grilled vegetables around the sauce and serve.

½ cup water

½ cup white or apple cider vinegar

2 teaspoons honey

1 teaspoon kosher salt

1 teaspoon whole black peppercorns

1 teaspoon mustard seeds

½ teaspoon red pepper flakes

1 bay leaf

1 medium red onion, thinly sliced

> **MAKE AHEAD:**
> The pickled onions will keep tightly covered in the refrigerator, for up to 2 weeks.

Pickled Red Onions

You will want to have a jar of tart pickled red onions on hand at all times since they are perfect complements to sandwiches, burgers, tacos, and many other dishes. They will keep in the refrigerator for weeks, so they're always ready to serve on a moment's notice.

Combine the water, vinegar, honey, salt, peppercorns, mustard seeds, red pepper flakes, and bay leaf in a small saucepan over high heat. Bring to a boil, stirring to dissolve the honey. Add the onion and stir. Lower the heat to medium and simmer for 1 minute. Remove from the heat and let the onions and brine cool in the pan.

Using tongs or a slotted spoon, transfer the onions to a clean 1-pint jar. Discard the bay leaf and pour the brine and the remaining solids over the onions, filling the jar. Gently tap the jar a few times to remove any air bubbles. Cover tightly and let cool to room temperature. Refrigerate for at least 2 hours before serving.

Billiards

Billiards is a broad family of cue sports including snooker and carom billiards, but in the United States usually refers specifically to pool games. Pool is played on a billiards table covered in felt with six pockets. But even proposing a game of pool is not so simple. There are many different styles of play and house rules sometimes vary depending where you're shooting.

Some of the more popular pool games include:

- 7-Ball
- 8-Ball
- 9-Ball
- 10-Ball

- Blackball
- Straight pool
- Bank pool
- 1-pocket

6 ounces green beans

1 garlic clove, thinly sliced

½ teaspoon whole black peppercorns

½ teaspoon coriander seeds

1 small dried chile

1 bay leaf

1 cup white vinegar

½ cup white wine

1 tablespoon sugar

1 teaspoon kosher salt

MAKE AHEAD: The pickled beans will keep, tightly covered in the refrigerator, for up to 1 month.

Pickled Green Beans

Quick-pickled green beans are a good thing to make during the summer months when fresh beans are abundant. These beans retain their crunch and are a welcome addition to any meal.

Before you trim the beans, arrange them vertically in a clean 1-pint jar to see how they will fit. Trim them to fit, leaving at least ½ inch of space at the top of the jar. Pack the trimmed beans back into the jar. Add the garlic, peppercorns, coriander seeds, chile, and bay leaf to the jar.

In a small saucepan over high heat, combine the vinegar, wine, sugar, and salt and bring to a boil, stirring to dissolve the salt and sugar. Remove from the heat.

Pour the brine over the beans, filling the jar to within ½ inch of the top. Gently tap the jar a few times to remove any air bubbles. Cover tightly and let cool to room temperature. Refrigerate for at least 1 day before serving.

Tennis Scoring

Though we're all probably used to it by now, do you ever stop to wonder why the scoring system in tennis is so . . . bizarre? After scoring one point, a player has a score of 15. At two points, the player reaches a score of 30. Alright, so scoring is worth 15 points? Well, no, since your third point raises your score to 40, not 45. Hm. This is made all the more complicated since you must lead by two points in tennis in order to win a game. Therefore, when both players reach 40, "40 all," they enter a Deuce. From there, a player who scores has Advantage. So now we're not even using numbers?

The origin of this unconventional scoring method is mostly lost to history, with the earliest references to similar calls traced to medieval France. Some theories suggest that clocks were used to conveniently keep track of score, with players advancing a quarter of the way (15 minutes) for each point, arriving at 60 after four points and winning the game. Along the way, 45 must have become 40. It's not a perfect theory though, since horologists will point out that it wasn't until the 1600s that clocks began to have minute hands.

Air Hockey

Air hockey owes its origins to a practical invention: the air table. The air table was developed to facilitate manufacturing, for instance, it allows people to pass lightweight material like cardboard over a large surface quickly and easily. It's the same technology that enables the air hockey puck to glide so smoothly and effortlessly across the playing surface.

Air hockey is popular across the globe, but especially so in the United States. The United States Air Hockey Association (USAA) is the largest governing body for the sport, with World Championship tournaments held each year. The competitions are dominated by American players. However, one other country has demonstrated exceptional skill. Venezuelan competitors have won first, second, and third place several times, while all other countries have failed to place in the top three since the organization's first championship in 1978.

1 fennel bulb, trimmed and sliced into thin quarters

1 garlic clove, thinly sliced

2 fresh thyme sprigs

2 fresh rosemary sprigs

1 teaspoon dried mixed herbs, such as fine herbs or herbes de Provençe

1 teaspoon whole black peppercorns

1 teaspoon fennel seed

¾ cup water

½ cup white or apple cider vinegar

1 tablespoon kosher salt

1 tablespoon sugar

> **MAKE AHEAD:** The pickled fennel will keep, tightly covered in the refrigerator, for up to 1 month.

Pickled Fennel

Fennel is a wonderful and versatile vegetable that tastes great when it is pickled. I like to toss it into salads and slaws and it is a terrific addition to an antipasto platter.

Put the fennel, garlic, fresh and dried herbs, peppercorns, and fennel seed in a clean 1-pint jar.

In a small saucepan over high heat, combine the water, vinegar, salt, and sugar and bring to a boil, stirring to dissolve the salt and sugar. Remove from the heat.

Pour the brine over the fennel mixture, filling the jar to within ½ inch of the top. Gently tap the jar a few times to remove any air bubbles. Cover tightly and let cool to room temperature. Refrigerate for at least 2 days before serving.

GAME DAY BUFFET

Whether you're interested in games, ads, or snacks, sports watch parties are always a good time to host friends and family and serve a rich and savory buffet of dishes that hit all the flavor notes.

Menu

SNACKS
- Herbed Bar Nuts (page 15)
- Deviled Eggs with Smoked Trout & Watercress (page 29)
- Kielbasa Bites with Red Wine & Orange Zest (page 47)

MAINS
- Gochujang Chicken Wings (page 67)
- Pulled Pork Sliders (page 68)
- Roasted Sweet Potato Fries (page 76)
- Cabbage & Fennel Coleslaw (page 79)

DESSERT
- Brownies (page 136)
- Blondies (page 137)

DRINKS
- Micheladas (page 159)
- Ginger-Lime Fizzes (page 165)

Game Plan

3 DAYS TO 1 MONTH AHEAD
Bake brownies and blondies. Store in airtight containers. They can be frozen for up to 1 month ahead of time.

1 WEEK AHEAD
Prepare the Ginger Simple Syrup (page 176) for the fizzes.

1 DAY AHEAD
Marinate and refrigerate the chicken wings.

Prepare and refrigerate the pulled pork.

Prepare and refrigerate the slaw.

Prepare a batch of Michelada mix and refrigerate.

DAY OF
Prepare the deviled eggs. Cook the eggs a few hours before serving and refrigerate. Fill the eggs about 1 hour before serving.

Roast the sweet potatoes for 1 hour 15 minutes before serving.

Cook the chicken wings 30 minutes before serving, keep warm in a low oven.

Heat the kielbasa bites and pulled pork for 15 minutes before serving.

Prepare the bar for drinks.

Assemble the sliders and serve.

TRIVIA & TACOS

Trivia games are fun for the whole family, and there's nothing more fun or delicious to serve to hungry players than a spread of tacos with a variety of fillings. You can assemble them yourself or, better yet, put all the fillings and garnishes out so that everyone can create and customize their own.

Menu

SNACKS
- Roasted Plum Tomato Salsa (page 38)
- Seafood Guacamole (page 39)

MAINS
- Barbecued Turkey Tacos (page 63)
- Shrimp Tacos with Cilantro-Lime Sauce (page 61)
- Black Bean & Spinach Tacos (page 64)

DESSERT
- Ice Cream Sundaes with Mexican Caramel Sauce (page 140)

DRINKS
- Sangria with Peaches & Strawberries (page 162)
- Agua Fresca (page 169)

Game Plan

1 WEEK AHEAD
Prepare and refrigerate the caramel sauce. Bring to room temperature and gently reheat before serving.

2 DAYS AHEAD
Prepare and refrigerate the barbecued turkey. Bring to room temperature before reheating.

Prepare and refrigerate the Agua Fresca. Stir well before serving.

1 DAY AHEAD
Prepare and refrigerate the salsa.

Prepare and refrigerate the cilantro-lime sauce.

DAY OF
Prepare and refrigerate the filling for the black bean tacos a few hours ahead of time.

Prepare and refrigerate the sangria a few hours before serving.

Prepare and assemble the taco garnishes.

Prepare the guacamole shortly before serving.

Prepare the bar for drinks.

Assemble and serve the shrimp tacos.

CHAPTER 3
BREADS, BRUSCHETTA & SANDWICHES

¼ cup golden raisins

¼ cup dry red wine

1 medium eggplant, cut into ½-inch rounds

1 large red onion, cut into ½-inch rounds

¼ cup olive oil for brushing

One 14.5-ounce can plum tomatoes

1½ tablespoons drained capers

½ cup pitted and chopped Kalamata olives

¼ cup pitted and chopped Spanish olives

1 jalapeño pepper, stemmed, seeded, and minced

1 tablespoon balsamic vinegar

2 tablespoons shredded basil leaves

2 tablespoons finely chopped flat-leaf parsley

Kosher salt and freshly ground pepper

2 flatbreads, homemade or store-bought

½ cup crumbled feta cheese

MAKE AHEAD:
The caponata will keep, covered in the refrigerator, for up to 1 week.

Roasted Vegetable Caponata Flatbreads

Caponata is one of those dishes you will want to make time and again—it's quite easy to prepare and yet its taste is complex enough to delight everyone. This version mixes the traditional Mediterranean flavors of eggplant, tomatoes, capers, olives, and fresh herbs with plumped golden raisins for a hint of sweetness. Serve it over warm flatbreads and top it with a crumble of feta cheese. You can make caponata a few days ahead of time—it gets better with a little time to mellow.

Put the raisins in a small saucepan and cover with the wine. Bring to a simmer over medium heat and cook for about 3 minutes. Set aside for the raisins to plump.

Preheat the oven to 400°F. Brush a large rimmed baking sheet with oil.

Arrange the eggplant and onion rounds on the sheet. They can overlap a bit. Brush the tops of the eggplant and onions with additional oil. Roast, turning once, until soft and lightly browned, 25 to 30 minutes. Set aside to cool.

Meanwhile, drain the juice from the tomatoes into a large mixing bowl. Chop the tomatoes and add to the bowl with the raisin mixture, capers, olives, and jalapeño pepper.

Chop the roasted eggplant and onion into coarse chunks, add to the tomato mixture, and stir. Add the vinegar, basil, and parsley and season with the salt and pepper. Toss gently, cover and let the mixture mellow for 6 to 8 hours or overnight in the refrigerator (see Make Ahead). Before serving, taste and adjust the seasoning, if necessary. Serve warm or room temperature.

Preheat the oven to 350°F and brush two rimmed baking sheets with oil.

Arrange the flatbreads on the baking sheets and brush the tops with olive oil. Bake for about 5 minutes. Flip the bread and bake for an additional 5 minutes until warmed through and slightly crusty.

Spoon the caponata over the bread, sprinkle with the feta cheese, cut into wedges, squares, or strips and serve.

CHIVE SPREAD

8 ounces cream cheese, at room temperature

1 shallot, minced

2 tablespoons minced chives, plus more for garnish

2 tablespoons drained capers, chopped

1 tablespoon fresh lemon juice

Dash of hot sauce (optional)

Kosher salt and freshly ground black pepper

Eight ½-inch-thick slices rye or pumpernickel bread, each cut in half

¼ cup (½ stick) unsalted butter, melted

5 ounces skinless smoked trout fillet, coarsely chopped (see Note)

Pickled Red Onions (page 82)

Toasts with Chive Spread, Smoked Trout & Pickled Onions

Smooth and creamy chive spread tastes great on crisp toasts topped with smoked trout and pickled onions. The spread yields a generous amount, so be sure to save the leftovers for slathering onto crackers or toasted bagels.

TO MAKE THE CHIVE SPREAD: Put the cream cheese, shallot, chives, capers, lemon juice, and hot sauce (if using) in a food processor and blend until smooth. Season with salt and pepper and blend again. Cover and refrigerate for up to 1 hour or overnight.

Preheat the oven to 425°F.

Arrange the bread slices on a baking sheet, brush one side of the bread with butter. Toast the bread, buttered sides up, until crisp, 6 to 8 minutes. Transfer toasts to a rack to cool.

Top each toast with the chive spread, smoked trout, and pickled red onions. Garnish with chives and serve.

Note: Smoked trout is available in fish markets and specialty markets where high-quality smoked fish is sold.

Go

Having originated in China more than 2,500 years ago, the abstract strategy game of Go is the oldest continuously played board game in the world. Often compared to chess, Go actually offers even more complexity and diversity of play from game to game. Played on a 19 x 19 grid containing 361 intersections and an equal number of playing tokens (called stones), there are a staggering number of unique board positions, estimated to be greater than the number of observable atoms in the universe!

Go is a game steeped in tradition. A traditional board is a free-standing floor board with supporting legs with players sitting on tatami mats. The most expensive and authentic sets have boards made from the wood of the Japanese kaya tree and stones fashioned from slate for black and clamshell for white.

Winning Poker Hands

1. **Royal flush:** A, K, Q, J, 10, all in the same suit.

2. **Straight flush:** Five cards in a sequence, all in the same suit.

3. **Four of a kind:** All four cards of the same rank.

4. **Full house:** Three of a kind with a pair.

5. **Flush:** Any five cards of the same suit, but not in a sequence.

6. **Straight:** Five cards in a sequence, but not of the same suit.

7. **Three of a kind:** Three cards of the same rank.

8. **Two pair:** Two different pairs.

9. **Pair:** Two cards of the same rank.

10. **High card:** When you haven't made any of the hands above, the highest card plays.

Six ½-inch slices country bread

About ½ cup olive oil for brushing

3 large garlic cloves, peeled and halved

Bruschetta

A big platter of bruschetta topped with any combination of ingredients is a great thing to serve on game night. There are so many tasty things to add to bruschetta—mozzarella, ricotta, or Parmesan cheese; vegetables like chopped tomatoes, grilled eggplant, fennel, sautéed spinach, or Swiss chard; savory cured meats such as prosciutto and salami. The combinations and possibilities are endless.

Bruschetta is traditionally made with thick slices of bread that are grilled or baked, brushed with olive oil, and rubbed with garlic. Be sure to use artisanal bread, such as ciabatta, sourdough, or baguettes for grilling.

Prepare the bruschetta according to the grill, grill pan, or oven directions that follow.

Cut each slice in half and serve with desired toppings.

Methods

GRILL METHOD: Prepare a medium-hot fire for direct grilling in a charcoal grill or preheat a gas grill to medium-high. Brush each side of the bread with olive oil. Arrange them in a single layer on the grill rack and grill, turning once, until they are golden brown and crispy and slightly charred around the edges, 2 to 3 minutes a side. Transfer to a platter and rub one side of each slice with a garlic half.

CONTINUED →

GRILL PAN METHOD: Heat a stove-top ungreased grill pan over medium heat. Brush each side of the bread with olive oil. Arrange them in a single layer on the pan and grill, turning once, until they are golden brown and crispy and slightly charred around the edges, 4 to 5 minutes a side. Transfer to a platter and rub one side of each slice with a garlic half.

OVEN METHOD: Preheat the oven to 450°F. Brush one side of the bread with olive oil. Arrange them in a single layer on a baking sheet and bake, turning once, until golden brown and crispy, about 3 minutes per side. Transfer to a platter and rub one side of each slice with a garlic half.

GAME FACT!

Names for Dice Rolls

Dice probably have their origins in ancient fortune-telling. Precursors to dice include knucklebones and two-sided throwing sticks. The six-sided dice we're most familiar with today descended from the ancient Romans. Since then, different playing cultures have come up with some fun names for specific dice combinations. Although many of these names were actually cooked up by craps dealers to break up the monotony of the game.

1 + 1:	Snake Eyes
6 + 6:	Boxcars or Midnight
6 + 2:	Easy Eight
5 + 5:	Speed Limit
4 + 4:	Hard Eight or Square Pair
4 + 3:	Big Red

2 tablespoons olive oil

3 cups baby spinach

One 15.5-ounce can chickpeas, rinsed and drained

2 tablespoons dry white wine

Pinch of red pepper flakes

Kosher salt and freshly ground black pepper

12 slices bruschetta (page 99)

BRUSCHETTA WITH WARM SPINACH & CHICKPEAS

Spinach and chickpeas are a delicious and winning combination for bruschetta. You can also improvise on the vegetarian beans and greens theme for these toasts—try Swiss chard and white beans, or watercress and black beans.

Heat 1 tablespoon of the olive oil in a skillet over medium heat. Add the spinach and sauté until wilted, about 3 minutes. Transfer to a bowl.

In the same pan, heat the remaining tablespoon of the olive oil, add the chickpeas, wine, and red pepper flakes. Season with salt and pepper and sauté until the wine is reduced and the chickpeas are cooked through, about 5 minutes.

Top each toast with warm spinach and chickpeas and serve.

CONTINUED →

MAKES 12 TOASTS;
SERVES 6 TO 8

2 tablespoons olive oil

3 large red bell peppers,
quartered, seeded, and
deveined

3 large yellow bell peppers,
quartered, seeded, and
deveined

Kosher salt

1 tablespoon balsamic
vinegar

12 slices bruschetta (page 99)

8 ounces mozzarella cheese,
thinly sliced

12 anchovy fillets

BRUSCHETTA WITH ROASTED BELL PEPPERS, MOZZARELLA & ANCHOVIES

Roasted bell peppers are always good to have on hand—they are a luscious addition to an antipasto platter and they make excellent toppings for sandwiches, burgers, and pizza. Here, they are served on bruschetta over slices of creamy mozzarella cheese and topped with anchovy fillets.

Preheat the oven to 350°F.

Brush a baking sheet with 1 tablespoon of the olive oil. Put the peppers, cut side down, on the baking sheet and sprinkle with salt.

Roast in the oven for 20 minutes, turn the peppers over and roast until softened and lightly browned, about another 20 minutes. Remove from the oven, drizzle the peppers with the vinegar and the remaining tablespoon of olive oil and toss lightly.

Top each toast with cheese, peppers, and an anchovy fillet and serve.

Other Bruschetta Ideas:

There are many delicious flavor combinations to use as toppings for bruschetta. Let what looks best at the market be your guide. Here are just a few suggestions:

- Roasted fennel, prosciutto, and Parmesan cheese
- Steamed asparagus, mozzarella cheese, and anchovies
- Grilled zucchini, toasted pine nuts, and chopped fresh mint
- Grilled eggplant, chopped fresh tomatoes, and basil
- Sautéed watercress and ham
- Sautéed broccoli rabe, mozzarella cheese, and salami
- Ricotta cheese, chopped fresh tomatoes, and basil
- Brie cheese and fig jam

Dreidel

One of the essential traditions of Hanukkah, spinning a dreidel is a fun, simple game of chance often played with children. Bets are usually placed with coins, candies, or chocolates in the center of the table. The players then take turns spinning and follow the instructions for the side that lands face up.

נ	**Nun:**	Lose your turn
ה	**He:**	Take half the pieces from the pot
ש	**Shin:**	Add one of your pieces to the pot
ג	**Gimel:**	Take everything from the pot!

Dominoes

Ancient precursors to dominoes date back to China in the 1100s. Since then, a whole world of domino games has evolved, especially in Asian and Latin American cultures.

Those of us who don't play dominoes might still enjoy playing with them. Apart from being used in tile games, dominoes are a great deal of fun to set up and knock down. It's all fun and games but of course some people have taken the art of triggering complex domino effects (known as domino shows) to serious levels.

Here are some world records:

- Most dominoes toppled in a circle: 89,995
- Longest domino wall: 40.14 meters, made of 42,173 dominoes
- Tallest domino structure: 30 feet 1.2 inches, made of 8,044 dominoes
- Most dominoes topped by an individual: 321,197

If you want to compete on the world stage of domino shows but don't want to buy thousands of them, you can still go for these:

- Most dominoes stacked on one vertical domino in 1 minute: 52
- Longest human domino line: 10,267 humans

TAPLENADE

3 tablespoons olive oil

2 anchovy fillets in oil

1 garlic clove, mashed to a paste

8 ounces pitted Kalamata olives, drained

2 tablespoons capers

1 tablespoon fresh lemon juice

1 teaspoon crushed thyme leaves

Kosher salt and freshly ground black pepper

PAN BAGNAT

One 16-inch baguette, halved lengthwise

4 ounces goat cheese, at room temperature

½ cup jarred roasted red peppers, cut into ¼-inch strips

2 hard-boiled eggs, thinly sliced crosswise

½ small red onion, thinly sliced lengthwise

2 cups shredded rotisserie chicken

1 cup loosely packed arugula

Roast Chicken Pan Bagnat

Pan bagnat (a French term that translates to "bathed bread") is a Provençal pressed sandwich that is usually made with tuna and tapenade. For a tasty twist on the classic, try it with shredded roast chicken. This sandwich should be made at least two to three hours before you plan to serve it, or you can make it up to a day ahead of time. This recipe can easily be doubled.

TO MAKE THE TAPENADE: Heat the olive oil in a small skillet over medium heat. Add the anchovies, and cook, stirring to break them up, for 2 minutes. Add the garlic, and cook until golden, about 2 minutes. Transfer the mixture to a food processor. Add the olives, capers, lemon juice, and thyme and blend until combined but still chunky. Transfer the tapenade to a bowl and season with salt and pepper.

TO ASSEMBLE THE SANDWICH: Spread the tapenade over the inside of both halves of the bread. Spread the goat cheese over the bottom half, followed by the pepper strips, egg slices, onion slices, chicken, and arugula. Cover with the top half of the bread and wrap the sandwich tightly in plastic wrap.

Put a large cast-iron skillet or another heavy object on top of the sandwich to weigh it down. Let the sandwich stand for at least 2 hours before serving or refrigerate overnight. Cut crosswise into six sandwiches and serve.

Who Invented the Sandwich?

Food historians generally agree that the sandwich was created by John Montagu, the Fourth Earl of Sandwich, a British statesman and notorious gambler. The story goes that in 1762 Montagu was on a gambling streak and didn't want to leave the gaming table to eat supper. He instructed a cook to prepare something that didn't require utensils that might interfere with his game. He was presented with sliced meat tucked between two slices of toast. Hence the sandwich was born!

A more likely story is that Montagu already knew about sandwiches from his excursions to the Mediterranean where he observed grilled pita breads and small sandwiches being served by Turks and Greeks and he understood its culinary convenience.

But since Montagu made the sandwich wildly popular among England's gentry, his title The Earl of Sandwich has prevailed, and today we still call "bread-enclosed convenience food" sandwiches.

ROMESCO SAUCE

1½ cups walnuts, toasted

¾ cup olive oil

1 tablespoon smoked paprika

1 teaspoon ancho chile powder

2 garlic cloves, peeled

One 16-ounce jar roasted red peppers, seeded and chopped

Kosher salt and freshly ground black pepper

Mayonnaise for serving

6 ciabatta rolls, halved lengthwise

2 pounds thinly sliced roast beef

Sandwich pickles for serving

Roast Beef & Romesco Sandwiches

Romesco sauce comes from Catalonia, Spain, where it is traditionally served as an accompaniment to grilled fish or meat. This rich and flavorful condiment is most often made with ground almonds or hazelnuts, but this version uses toasted walnuts. It tastes terrific with rare roast beef.

TO MAKE THE ROMESCO SAUCE: Combine the walnuts, oil, paprika, chile powder, garlic, and peppers in a food processor and blend until coarsely ground. Season with salt and pepper and blend again. Set the romesco aside (see Make Ahead).

TO ASSEMBLE THE SANDWICHES: Spread the mayonnaise on the bottoms of the rolls; top with roast beef, pickles, romesco sauce, and the tops of the rolls.

> **MAKE AHEAD:**
> The romesco sauce will keep, covered in the refrigerator, for up to 1 week.

Risk

A game of strategy, chance, and ruthless world conquest, Risk is a classic known for its marathon-style gameplay. Invented in 1959 and published by Hasbro, Risk also offers an interesting window into popular culture over the years through its many licensed versions. You can see a progression of popular mainstream science-fiction and fantasy franchises that offer unique worlds and settings for a game of territorial domination. Some of these include:

- Risk: The Lord of the Rings (2002)
- Risk: Star Wars Trilogy Edition (2006)
- Risk Junior: Narnia (2006)
- Risk: Transformers Edition (2007)
- Risk: Halo Wars (2009)
- Risk: Metal Gear Solid (2011)
- Risk: The Walking Dead Survival Edition (2013)
- Risk: Plants Vs Zombies (2013)
- Risk: Doctor Who (2013)
- Risk: Game of Thrones (2015)
- Risk: Marvel Cinematic Universe (2015)
- Risk: Star Trek 50th Anniversary Edition (2016)
- Risk: Rick and Morty (2018)

Catan

Catan, also known as Settlers of Catan, is a multiplayer strategy game themed after settling land and managing natural resources. It was developed in the 1990s by German designer Klaus Teuber and released in 1995. Catan is widely popular across the globe and it is one of the most famous and mainstream German-style board games or Eurogames. The Eurogame movement boomed in the 2010s, with games like Catan, Carcassonne, and Ticket to Ride being played in many board game cafes opening across the United States.

Much like Risk or Monopoly, there are many licensed versions of Catan, speaking to its mainstream appeal:

- Catan Starfarers
- Catan Junior
- Catan Family Edition
- Catan Settlers of America
- Catan Merchants of Europe
- Catan Histories Rise of the Inkas
- Star Trek Catan
- A Game of Thrones Catan: Brotherhood of the Watch

6 tablespoons (¾ stick)
unsalted butter, at room
temperature

2 tablespoons finely minced
dill

16 slices thin white sandwich
bread

3 small cucumbers, peeled
and very thinly sliced

¼ to ½ pound smoked
salmon, thinly sliced

8 sprigs fresh watercress,
plus 4 for garnish

Smoked Salmon & Cucumber Tea Sandwiches with Dill Butter

Elegant and easy, tea sandwiches are delightful to serve for a small get-together. Of course, they are just the thing to nibble on with a cup of tea, but a glass of champagne is not a bad pairing either.

In a small bowl, mix the butter and dill together with a fork.

Remove the crusts from the bread. Spread the butter on half of the slices of bread. Top with cucumbers, smoked salmon, and a sprig of watercress. Put a slice of bread on top and gently press down on each sandwich.

Cut each sandwich on the diagonal into four triangles. Cover and let chill in the refrigerator for up to 3 hours before serving. To serve, arrange the sandwiches on a platter and garnish with watercress sprigs.

Pictionary

Since it was first published in 1985, Pictionary has had five categories for its drawing prompts: Person/Place/Animal, Object, Action, Difficult, and All Play. Of course, when you're rolling the dice we all hope anything, *anything* other than Difficult. And once you inevitably land on a Difficult square and draw the card, you pray that the word in green isn't *too* difficult. Will the Pictionary gods be merciful? Over the years, some truly tough prompts have been buried in that stack of cards, ready to confound unlucky drawers and guessers. Below are some examples of the worst of the worst. See if you and your guests have what it takes. How would you draw these?

- Ridge
- Suds
- Caffeine
- Uniform
- Shaft
- Master Key
- Candlestick
- Stained Glass
- Walk the Plank
- Slack
- Bon Voyage
- Math
- Broken
- Alfalfa

- Loud
- Warm
- Musk
- Gallery
- Clear
- Bakery
- Willow
- Hide
- Proposal
- Bad
- Bottle Top
- Beauty Pageant
- Radiation
- Cavalry

- Brunch
- On the Way
- Penitentiary
- Rearview Mirror
- Solo
- Denim
- Audience
- Story
- Takeoff
- Appliance
- Penny
- Team

6 hard-boiled eggs, peeled

2 bunches fresh watercress,
stems removed, reserving
12 sprigs for garnish

¼ cup chopped fresh chives

¼ to ½ cup mayonnaise

½ teaspoon Dijon mustard

Kosher salt and freshly
ground black pepper

Dash of hot sauce

16 slices thin white or
whole wheat bread, or a
combination

MAKE AHEAD:
The egg salad will
keep, covered in
the refrigerator,
for up to 1 day.
Taste and adjust
the seasoning, if
necessary, before
preparing the
sandwiches.

Egg Salad & Watercress Tea Sandwiches

Egg salad is a favorite sandwich staple that is wonderful to use in tea sandwiches. I like to include fresh watercress and chives for added color and taste. You can also take it further and add any number of ingredients, such as chopped ham, bacon, or smoked salmon, and other herbs, to the egg salad mix.

Finely chop the eggs, watercress, and chives and transfer to a large bowl. Mix the mayonnaise and mustard together in a small bowl and add just enough to the eggs to moisten and bind the mixture. Season with salt, pepper, and hot sauce and gently mix together (see Make Ahead).

Remove the crusts from the bread. Spread the egg and watercress mixture on half of the slices of bread. Put a slice of bread on top and gently press down on each sandwich.

Cut each sandwich on the diagonal into four triangles. Serve immediately or cover and let chill in the refrigerator for up to 3 hours. To serve, arrange the sandwiches on a platter and garnish with watercress sprigs.

1 tablespoon kosher salt

2 lemons, halved

3 bay leaves

3 sprigs fresh thyme

3 sprigs fresh parsley

¼ cup Old Bay Seasoning

2 pounds large shrimp,
unpeeled

½ cup finely chopped red
onion

⅔ cup chopped celery

1 cup mayonnaise

2 teaspoons fresh lemon
juice

2 tablespoons chopped fresh
tarragon

2 tablespoons chopped fresh
parsley

Kosher salt and freshly
ground black pepper

16 slider (mini hamburger)
rolls or 8 regular
hamburger rolls, split

Shrimp Salad Sliders

Shrimp salad never disappoints, and whenever I serve
a plate piled high with shrimp salad sliders I'm amazed
at how quickly they disappear. In this recipe the shrimp
is poached in boiling water with the addition of lemons,
fresh herbs, and a generous amount of Old Bay Seasoning. The flavor is fantastic.

Fill a large pot with water. Add the salt, squeeze the lemon
juice into the water and add the lemon halves. Add the bay
leaves, thyme and parsley sprigs, and seasoning. Bring to
a boil over high heat.

Reduce the heat to medium and add the shrimp. Simmer,
uncovered, until the shrimp turn bright pink and their
tails curl, 3 to 5 minutes. Using a slotted spoon, transfer
the shrimp from the poaching liquid to a colander and let
drain. Do not rinse. Chill the shrimp thoroughly.

Peel, devein, and chop the shrimp and transfer to a
large bowl. Add the red onion and celery and gently toss
together.

Whisk the mayonnaise and lemon juice together in a
medium bowl. Add the tarragon and chopped parsley and
whisk again. Season with salt and pepper. Add the mayonnaise mixture to the shrimp and gently toss together
until combined. Cover and refrigerate for at least 1 hour
before serving.

Spoon the shrimp salad onto the bottom halves of the
rolls, dividing it evenly. Replace the tops of the rolls; if
using regular hamburger rolls, cut each sandwich in half.
Serve immediately.

Two-Letter Scrabble Words

While laying down OXYPHENBUTAZONE for the theoretical highest-possible score of 1,778 points would feel incredible, it isn't very likely to happen. In fact, knowing the more than 100 two-letter words in the Scrabble dictionary is far more useful to players.

Below is the full list, along with some definitions to impress your opponents when they inevitably doubt your word is real.

- AA (basaltic lava having a rough, broken surface), AB, AD, AE, AG, AH, AI (a three-toed sloth), AL, AM, AN, AR, AS, AT, AW, AX, AY
- BA, BE, BI, BO, BY
- DA, DE, DO
- ED, EF, EH, EL (an elevated railway), EM, EN, ER, ES, ET, EW, EX
- FA, FE
- GI (a white garment worn in martial arts), GO
- HA, HE, HI, HM, HO
- ID, IF, IN, IS, IT
- JO (sweetheart, dear—often used in addressing a person)
- KA, KI
- LA (sixth note of the major scale), LI, LO
- MA, ME, MI, MM, MO, MU (twelfth letter of the Greek alphabet), MY
- NA, NE, NO, NU
- OD, OE, OF, OH, OI, OK, OM (a mantra consisting of the sound \'ōm\ and used in contemplation of ultimate reality), ON, OP, OR, OS (bone), OW, OX, OY
- PA, PE (17th letter of the Hebrew alphabet), PI, PO
- QI
- RE
- SH (used often in prolonged or rapidly repeated form to urge or command silence or less noise), SI, SO
- TA (British—thanks), TE, TI, TO
- UH, UM, UN, UP, US, UT
- WE, WO
- XI, XU (a coin formerly minted by South Vietnam equivalent to the cent)
- YA, YE, YO
- ZA (slang—pizza)

A Timeline of Chess

The origins of chess can be traced to the Indian strategy game chaturanga in the 7th century. Since then, the game has evolved in a number of fascinating ways through the present day.

900s: Light and dark squares are introduced.

1200s: Pawns are permitted to move two spaces on their first moves.

1471:   The first-ever book entirely about chess is published.

1575:   The first-known international chess championship takes place in Madrid.

1620:   In response to the maturation of the queen and bishop into powerful pieces, castling is developed as a way to move the king to safety.

1769:   The Mechanical Turk, a fake chess playing machine, is created to impress the Empress of Austria. In fact, a skilled human player operated the machine from within. Still, the hoax endured for more than 80 years, touring around Europe and defeating most opponents.

1849:   The Staunton chess set, designed by Nathaniel Cooke, is released and quickly becomes the world's standard. Today, this style is required at all serious competitions.

1886:   The first official World Chess Championship is held.

1924:   Fédération Internationale des Échecs (FIDE) is established in Switzerland and becomes the governing body of organized chess.

1950:   FIDE introduces the Grandmaster title.

1972:   The World Chess Championship concludes with Bobby Fischer (US) defeating Boris Spassky (USSR) in a final seen as a Cold War confrontation.

1996:   Chess-playing supercomputer Deep Blue defeats World Champion Garry Kasparov in a match.

SNACKS & SANDWICHES FOR GAME NIGHTS

Whether you're getting together for a lively poker night, a fierce Monopoly marathon, or a Scrabble tournament, you will surely get hungry. A tray of snacks and a big platter of hearty sandwiches will please all the players.

Menu

SNACKS
- Hot & Sweet Chex Mix (page 19)
- Roasted Onion & Shallot Dip (page 33) with crudités and chips

MAINS
- Roast Chicken **Pan Bagnat** (page 105)
- **Roast Beef & Romesco Sandwiches (page 107)**
- Shrimp Salad Sliders (page 114)
- Pickled Red Onions (page 82)
- Pickled Green Beans (page 84)
- Pickled Fennel (page 87)

DESSERT
- Chocolate Chip–Peanut Butter Cookies (page 139)

DRINKS
- Nor'easter Cocktail (page 152)
- Iced Orange & Ginger Tea (page 170)

Game Plan

2 WEEKS AHEAD

Prepare the chex mix. It can be stored in an airtight container for up to 2 weeks.

Prepare and refrigerate the pickled vegetables. They can be stored in the refrigerator for up to 2 weeks.

1 WEEK AHEAD

Prepare and refrigerate the romesco sauce. It can be stored in the refrigerator for up to 1 week.

3 DAYS AHEAD

Prepare and refrigerate the onion dip. It can be stored in the refrigerator for up to 3 days.

1 DAY AHEAD

Prepare the pan bagnat and refrigerate.

Bake the cookies. They can be stored in an airtight container for up to 1 day ahead.

Prepare the crudités and store in the refrigerator.

Prepare and refrigerate the iced tea.

DAY OF

Prepare and refrigerate the shrimp salad a few hours before serving.

Prepare and arrange the sandwiches about a half hour before serving.

Prepare the bar for drinks.

CHAPTER 4
DESSERTS & TREATS

POUND CAKE

Cooking spray and sugar for
coating the pan

2¾ cups unbleached
all-purpose flour

½ teaspoon baking soda

¾ teaspoon kosher salt

½ pound (2 sticks)
unsalted butter, at room
temperature

2½ cups sugar

1 teaspoon pure vanilla
extract

2 tablespoons grated lemon
zest

5 large eggs, at room
temperature

1 cup sour cream

½ cup fresh lemon juice

LEMON GLAZE

½ cup sugar

½ cup fresh lemon juice

BERRIES

½ pint fresh strawberries,
hulled and sliced

½ pint fresh blueberries

½ pint fresh raspberries

1 to 2 teaspoons superfine
sugar

Lemon Pound Cake with Fresh Berries

This is a wonderful lemon cake recipe to have on hand. It's the perfect cake to serve with fresh berries for dessert, and it tastes even better after a day or two or three. Be sure to glaze the cake while it is still warm.

Position an oven rack in the center of the oven and preheat the oven to 350°F. Spray the inside of a 10-inch Bundt pan with cooking spray and sprinkle with sugar, tapping out the excess.

In a medium bowl, combine the flour, baking soda, and salt and set aside.

In the bowl of an electric mixer set on medium-high speed or with a hand mixer, beat the butter and 2½ cups sugar until smooth and creamy. Add the vanilla and lemon zest and mix well. Add the eggs one at a time, mixing well after each addition. Scrape down the sides of the bowl.

Mix the sour cream and ½ cup lemon juice together. Add about a third of the flour mixture to the batter and beat to incorporate. Add a third of the sour cream mixture and beat again. Add the remaining flour and sour cream to the batter, in alternating thirds. Spoon the batter into the prepared pan.

Bake for 1 hour, or until a toothpick or cake tester inserted in the cake comes out clean. Let the cake cool in the pan for 5 minutes. Run a sharp thin knife around the inside of the pan and the tube, then cover with a wire rack and invert. Lift the pan from the cake, leaving it upside down. Place the rack over a large piece of foil or wax paper and prepare the glaze.

CONTINUED →

TO MAKE THE GLAZE: Mix the 1/2 cup sugar and 1/2 cup lemon juice together. Add a bit of water if the glaze seems too thick. Pour the glaze over the top of the cake and let cool completely. It is best to wait a few hours (or even a day) before cutting the cake.

Combine the strawberries, blueberries, and raspberries in a bowl and sprinkle with the superfine sugar. Let the berries macerate for about 1/2 hour before serving.

Spoon the berries over each slice of cake and serve.

OLIVE OIL CAKE

1¼ cups olive oil, plus oil for the pan

2 cups unbleached all-purpose flour

1¾ cups sugar

1½ teaspoons kosher salt

½ teaspoon baking soda

½ teaspoon baking powder

1¼ cups whole milk

3 large eggs, at room temperature

2 teaspoons grated orange zest

¼ cup fresh orange juice

¼ cup Grand Marnier

LEMON CRÈME FRAÎCHE

One 7-ounce container crème fraîche

¼ cup sugar

Juice of 1 lemon

½ teaspoon lemon zest

1 teaspoon pure vanilla extract

MAKE AHEAD:
The cake and the crème fraîche can be made up to 2 days ahead of time.

Olive Oil Cake with Lemon Crème Fraîche

This rich and aromatic cake is a snap to make and there is no need to use a mixer or a food processor. It's simply a blend of flour, sugar, and other dry ingredients whisked together with eggs and olive oil. It's a good cake to serve on its own, but it's even better with a dollop of lemon crème fraîche. Plan to make it ahead of time—because it tastes great and gets a little boozy after two or three days.

Position an oven rack in the center of the oven and preheat the oven to 350°F. Oil a 9-inch round cake pan that is at least 2 inches deep and line the bottom with parchment paper.

In a medium bowl, whisk the flour, sugar, salt, baking soda, and baking powder together. In a large mixing bowl, whisk the olive oil, milk, eggs, orange zest, orange juice, and Grand Marnier together. Add the flour mixture and whisk until just combined. The batter will be a bit thin.

Pour the batter into the prepared pan and bake for 55 minutes to 1 hour, until the top is golden brown and a toothpick or cake tester inserted in the center of the cake comes out clean. Transfer the cake to a rack and let cool for 30 minutes.

Run a sharp knife around the edges of the pan, invert the cake onto the rack, peel off the paper, and let cool completely.

TO MAKE THE LEMON CRÈME FRAÎCHE: Whisk the crème fraîche, sugar, lemon juice, lemon zest, and vanilla together until well combined. Cover and chill in the refrigerator until ready to serve (see Make Ahead).

THE HISTORY OF CLUE

Clue was introduced in the United States in 1949, and to this day it is still a perennial favorite of board game players all over the world. In this game of mystery, players must move from room to room in a mansion to figure out who murdered the victim—the unfortunately named Mr. Boddy—as well as the room of the crime and the weapon that was used. Was it Miss Scarlett in the library with a candlestick? Or Professor Plum in the conservatory with a revolver? The story of the invention of Clue is as interesting as the game itself.

In the early 1940s, a British musician named Anthony Pratt was watching murder-mystery games being acted out in elegant country mansions, where he played the piano at parties. Pratt took notes as guests playacted crimes that involved fake murders replete with melodramatic screaming and falling to the floor.

During World War II, Pratt re-created those murder mystery games in miniature as a board game called Murder! The longtime Birmingham resident, who then worked in a local arms factory during the war, invented the suspects and weapons around 1943 as a way that he and his wife, Elva, could pass the time during long nights of air-raid blackouts. Slowly their idea evolved into a board game that they designed on their dining room table. Pratt filed for a patent for the game in 1944 and it was granted in 1947. Pratt went on to sell it to the UK games manufacturer Waddington's. Because of war shortages, the game wasn't actually released until 1948. Its original name was Cluedo, a mash-up of *clue* and *Ludo*, the name of a 19th-century board game that's Latin for "I Play." After Parker Brothers acquired the rights to the game in 1949, it was renamed Clue since Ludo was unfamiliar to Americans.

In Pratt's original version of the game there were 10 characters: Doctor Black, Mr. Brown, Mr. Gold, the Reverend Mister Green, Miss Grey, Professor Plum, Miss Scarlett, Nurse White, Mrs. Silver, and Colonel Yellow. But to simplify the game, they were eventually whittled down to six. As well, Colonel Yellow's name was changed to Colonel Mustard.

There have been many changes and updates to the Clue characters and their weapons over the years, and one of the most significant was the killing off of Mrs. White in 2016. It is the first time a game character has been permanently retired. Hasbro (now owners of Parker Brothers) replaced her with the younger and more accomplished Dr. Orchid, the adopted daughter of the mansion's owner. She is a working scientist with a PhD, but, alas, she comes with a sinister past.

Today, Clue is still wildly popular. Because of its broad appeal it is played by adults and children all over the world. Its place in the pantheon of board games comes right after chess, checkers, Monopoly, and Scrabble.

The (Checkered) Game of Life

Go to college or jump straight into your career? Buy a Tudor-style house or a camper-trailer? Retire at Millionaire Estates or Countryside Acres? These are the dilemmas we're used to facing when we play The Game of Life, a roll-and-move style board game where we can live out our fantasy of marriage, kids, and curing the common cold. Most people think the Game of Life first came around in the 1960s—and this is true for the game's current format. However, its origins lie deeper in the past, all the way in the 19th century.

Milton Bradley himself created the predecessor to the beloved classic in 1860. The game was then called The Checkered Game of Life. It was indeed played on a checkered board, but the name was also a pun on the sometimes indecent nature of life. The original game is a bit more serious than its modern incarnation, inspired by "morality" games popular at the time that were used to give children religious or ethical instruction.

Squares you could land on included: Honesty, Industry, Bravery, Fame, Wealth, and Happy Old Age. All sounds pretty good, you might say. Well, there are some less pleasant squares as well, including: Poverty, Crime, Intemperance, Disgrace, and Prison. Oof. Some squares are a little more ambiguous, at least to a modern player's sensibilities. These include: Congress, Speculation, and Fat Office. Well, life is what you make it.

CUPCAKES

**2 cups unbleached
all-purpose flour**

2 teaspoons baking soda

1½ cups vegetable oil

2 cups sugar

**4 large eggs, at room
temperature**

**1 tablespoon ground
cinnamon**

½ teaspoon ground ginger

¼ teaspoon ground cloves

1 teaspoon kosher salt

**3 cups finely grated carrots
(about 4 large carrots)**

**2½ cups pecans, toasted and
chopped**

FROSTING

**¼ pound (1 stick)
unsalted butter, at room
temperature**

**One 8-ounce package
cream cheese, at room
temperature**

1 cup confectioners' sugar

**2 teaspoons pure vanilla
extract**

Pinch of salt

Carrot Cake Cupcakes with Cream Cheese Frosting

These cupcakes are made with fresh carrots, spices, and toasted pecans, and they have a nice light taste and texture. I highly recommend grating the carrots in a food processor.

Position an oven rack in the center of the oven and preheat the oven to 400°F. Line two muffin pans with paper liners.

In a medium bowl, mix the flour and baking soda together and set aside.

Using an electric mixer on medium speed, beat the oil, sugar, eggs, cinnamon, ginger, cloves, and salt together in a large bowl until smooth. Add the flour mixture and stir until smooth. Add the grated carrots and pecans and stir until just blended. Spoon the batter into the muffin cups until each is three-quarters full. Bake for 10 minutes then reduce the oven temperature to 350°F and bake 25 to 30 minutes, or until a toothpick or a cake tester inserted in the center of the cakes comes out clean. Cool them on a rack.

TO MAKE THE FROSTING: In a large bowl with an electric mixer on medium speed, beat the butter and cream cheese together until smooth. Add the sugar, vanilla, and salt and beat until very smooth. Frost the cupcakes generously and serve.

Dartboards

Dartboards are a common sight in pubs and taverns across the world, particularly in the United States and United Kingdom. The point values around the board are designed to penalize players for inaccuracy, with high-value areas—like the Triple 20—surrounded by low-scoring zones. In the early 20th century, boards were often made of wood and would be replaced when the Triple 20 suffered too much wear.

Butter and flour to coat the baking pan

1 cup unbleached all-purpose flour

1 teaspoon baking powder

½ cup (1 stick) unsalted butter, at room temperature

½ cup firmly packed light brown sugar

½ cup plus 3 tablespoons granulated sugar

2 large eggs, at room temperature

2½ cups ripe peaches (about 3 peaches), peeled and thinly sliced

1 cup fresh blueberries

½ teaspoon ground cinnamon

Blueberry & Peach Squares

This cake is at its best when the fresh blueberries and ripe summer peaches are at their peak. It's so easy to serve since it's simply cut into squares and eaten out of hand. You might want to double the recipe—this cake goes fast.

Position an oven rack in the center of the oven and preheat the oven to 350°F. Lightly butter and flour an 8-inch square baking pan.

Whisk together the flour and baking powder in a medium bowl.

Using an electric mixer on high speed, cream the butter, brown sugar, and ½ cup of the granulated sugar in a large bowl until light and fluffy, about 3 minutes. With the mixer running on medium speed, add the flour mixture to the batter a little at a time; do not overmix. Beat in the eggs.

Scrape the batter into the prepared pan. Smooth the surface and then arrange the sliced peaches and blueberries on top of the batter.

Combine the remaining 3 tablespoons sugar with the cinnamon in a small bowl and sprinkle the mixture over the peaches.

Bake for about 1 hour, until a toothpick or cake tester inserted in the center of the cake comes out clean and the cake begins to pull away from the sides of the pan. Remove the cake from the oven and cool in the pan on a wire rack. When completely cool, serve the cake directly from the pan or remove it from the pan, cut it into squares, and serve.

Dungeons and Dragons

D&D has had a long and tumultuous history. After the fantasy role-playing game was created in the 1970s, it exploded in popularity and became a symbol of nerd culture. After having gone through some dark times, including a Satanic moral scare in the 1980s and 90s, D&D is now more popular than ever. Especially during the COVID pandemic, many began to play D&D as a way to connect with friends virtually.

Want to get into it? It can be a little intimidating, but it's really all about letting your imagination take over. Take a look at these character classes and see if any inspire you to pick up the D20 and get rolling:

- Barbarian
- Bard
- Cleric
- Druid
- Fighter
- Monk
- Paladin
- Ranger
- Rogue
- Sorcerer
- Warlock
- Wizard

CAKE

Butter and flour to coat the baking pan

1¼ cups unbleached all-purpose flour

1 teaspoon baking powder

Pinch of salt

½ cup (1 stick) unsalted butter, at room temperature, cut into pieces

1 cup sugar

2 large eggs, at room temperature, separated

½ cup whole milk

1 cup chopped walnuts

1 teaspoon pure vanilla extract

SAUTÉED PEARS

2 tablespoons unsalted butter

6 small Bosc pears, cored, peeled, and cut into ¼-inch pieces

2 tablespoons brown sugar

1 tablespoon ground cinnamon

1 teaspoon ground nutmeg

2 tablespoons fresh lemon juice

CREAM

1 cup heavy cream

1 tablespoon sugar

1 teaspoon ground cinnamon

Walnut Cake with Sautéed Pears and Cinnamon Cream

This easy and delicious cake is so good topped with spice-infused sautéed pears and whipped cream.

Position an oven rack in the center of the oven and preheat the oven to 350°F. Lightly butter and flour a 9-inch round cake pan and tap out the excess flour.

Combine the flour, baking powder, and salt in a medium bowl and whisk 8 to 10 times until well mixed.

Using an electric mixer set on medium-high speed, cream ½ cup butter and sugar together in a large bowl. Add the egg yolks and beat until smooth. Add the flour mixture in three or four batches, alternating with the milk and ending with the dry ingredients. Stir well and fold in the nuts and vanilla.

Using an electric mixer set on medium-high speed, beat the egg whites until they hold stiff peaks. Fold the whites into the batter just until mixed. Spread the batter in the cake pan. Bake 35 to 40 minutes, or until the top is golden brown and a toothpick or cake tester inserted in the center of the cake comes out clean.

TO PREPARE THE PEARS: In a sauté pan or skillet, melt 2 tablespoons butter over medium-high heat and cook the pears, stirring, for about 5 minutes, or just until softened. Sprinkle with the brown sugar. Add 1 tablespoon cinnamon, the nutmeg, and the lemon juice and mix well. Cover to keep warm.

TO MAKE THE CREAM: Using an electric mixer set on medium-high speed, whip the cream and 1 tablespoon sugar until the cream is thick but not dry. Add 1 teaspoon cinnamon and continue whipping until the cream is the desired consistency. Serve the cake topped with the pears and cream.

6 tablespoons (¾ stick)
unsalted butter, at room
temperature

1 cup sugar

1 egg, at room temperature

1¼ cups unbleached
all-purpose flour

4 ounces almonds, ground

1½ tablespoons fresh lemon
juice

> **MAKE AHEAD:**
> The cookies will
> keep, covered in an
> airtight container,
> for up to 3 days.

Luscious Lemon Wafers

I like to serve these crisp and delicious cookies with ice cream or sorbet. They keep beautifully in an airtight container until they're ready to serve.

Position an oven rack in the center of the oven and preheat the oven to 350°F. Lightly butter two baking sheets.

In a large bowl, with an electric mixer on medium speed, beat the butter, sugar, and egg until smooth.

Stir in the flour, almonds, and lemon juice and mix until well combined.

Spoon the dough onto the baking sheets then press the dough into 2½-inch rounds with floured fingers.

Bake for 10 to 12 minutes, or until the edges are lightly browned. Remove the cookies with a spatula and cool on racks (see Make Ahead).

MAHJONG

There are many stories and theories about the origins of mahjong, and most of them are unsubstantiated. Like many popular games, its true history doesn't seem to have one clear beginning.

An often-told yet unlikely story is that mahjong was created in China by Confucius. Throughout China's history, many games were invented and played that were similar to modern mahjong. These early games used wood and ivory cards similar to today's mahjong tiles. After centuries of evolving game cards and strategies, it is thought by many that the game we now know as mahjong was ultimately created in the mid- to late 19th century. However, there is still some debate on who's responsible for its creation.

The game was played in China and as it became more popular it spread outside of China's borders and into other Asian countries. Mahjong was probably first introduced to Westerners around the turn of the 20th century when people began playing it in British clubs in Shanghai.

Mahjong was introduced to America by Joseph P. Babcock, who worked for the Standard Oil Company. He began importing sets to the U.S. from China in 1922 and the popularity of the game in the United States grew rapidly. Babcock published a new, simpler set of rules (there were no official written rules in China at the time) and several companies, such as Milton Bradley and Parker Brothers, created game sets. The craze grew all over the country, but it was most popular in New York City where the National Mah Jongg League was eventually created.

How It's Played

Mahjong is a game for four players. A set of 144 mahjong tiles consists of 36 tiles in the Bamboo suit, 36 in the Circle suit, 36 in the Character suit, 16 Wind tiles, 12 Dragon tiles and 8 bonus tiles (4 Flowers and 4 Seasons). One thing to remember is that there are about as many variations of mahjong as there are suits and sets of tiles. When playing a game of mahjong, it's important that all four players are all playing by the same rules.

Although it appears initially to be a very complicated game, it is effectively played like the card game rummy. The aim is to collect sets of tiles according to the number and type shown on the face of each tile. A player takes and discards a tile each turn, and the first player who gets a winning "legal hand" made up of 14 tiles wins or goes "mahjong."

The game is quite simple when it's reduced to its basics, but accompanying rituals and complex scoring change this. One of these rituals, the process of shuffling the tiles at the start of the game, is known as "the twittering of the sparrows." Since the word *mahjong* means "the game of the sparrows" in Chinese, it seems likely that this is the source of the game's name.

The Social Aspect of Mahjong

The beauty of mahjong is that it's meant to be shared, and the social aspect of it is very important to those who play it. Playing it can be a form of escape, but at the same time many friendships are formed and sustained at the mahjong table. It's a great opportunity to chat, eat, drink, and play together.

Brownies

MAKES 16 BROWNIES; SERVES 6 TO 8

4 ounces unsweetened chocolate

½ cup (1 stick) unsalted butter, at room temperature

1⅓ cups sugar

½ teaspoon pure vanilla extract

3 large eggs, at room temperature

¾ cup unbleached all-purpose flour

½ cup chopped walnuts or pecans

MAKE AHEAD:
Fully cooled brownies will keep, covered in an airtight container, for up to 5 days. They can be frozen for up to 1 month.

Brownies are irresistible, and this recipe will not disappoint. They are fudgy on the inside and the tops have nice crackly crusts. You may want to double the recipe and bake them in a larger (8-by-16-inch) pan.

Position an oven rack in the center of the oven and preheat the oven to 325°F. Lightly butter an 8-inch square pan.

Melt the chocolate and butter in the top of a double boiler placed over simmering water. Set aside to cool for 5 minutes.

Put the sugar in a medium bowl and pour in the chocolate mixture. Using an electric mixer on medium speed, mix until blended. Scrape the bowl with a rubber spatula.

Add the vanilla. With the mixer on low speed, add the eggs one at a time, blending well after each addition.

Add the flour on low speed, then finish mixing by hand, making sure the batter is well incorporated. Stir in the nuts.

Transfer the batter to the pan and spread evenly. Bake the brownies until a thin crust forms on the top and a toothpick or cake tester comes out clean, about 35 minutes. Let the brownies cool in the pan on a rack for 1 hour before cutting them. They are best served the next day (see Make Ahead).

½ cup (1 stick) unsalted butter

½ cup light brown sugar

½ cup dark brown sugar

2 large eggs, at room temperature

1½ teaspoons pure vanilla extract

1 cup cake flour (not self-rising)

¼ teaspoon kosher salt

⅓ cup chopped pecans

MAKE AHEAD:
Fully cooled blondies will keep, covered in an airtight container, for up to 5 days. They can be frozen for up to 1 month.

Blondies

These rich blondies have a nice cake-like texture with a great flavor. They are fantastic with vanilla ice cream or frozen yogurt. They can also be cut into very small squares and served with toothpicks as small bites.

Position an oven rack in the center of the oven and preheat the oven to 325°F. Lightly butter an 8-inch square pan.

Using a hand mixer, beat the butter and sugars together in a large bowl until fluffy, 2 to 3 minutes. Add the eggs, one at a time, blending well after each addition. Stir in the vanilla. Add the flour and salt and beat until well mixed. Fold in the pecans. Pour the batter into the prepared pan and smooth the top.

Transfer the batter to the pan and spread evenly. Bake until a thin crust forms on the top and a toothpick or cake tester comes out clean, 30 to 35 minutes. Let cool in the pan on a rack for 1 hour before cutting them (see Make Ahead).

1½ cups unbleached
all-purpose flour

1 teaspoon baking soda

¼ teaspoon kosher salt

1 cup firmly packed dark
brown sugar

4 tablespoons (½ stick)
unsalted butter, at room
temperature

¼ cup coconut oil

1 large egg plus 1 large egg
yolk, at room temperature

½ teaspoon pure vanilla
extract

1 cup smooth peanut butter

1½ cups (9 ounces) chocolate
chips

Chocolate Chip–Peanut Butter Cookies

A plate of these heavenly cookies served warm from the oven will keep everyone's energy level up during a hard-fought game of Monopoly, Risk, or Clue. They should be served with glasses of ice cold milk.

Position the oven racks in the center of the oven and preheat the oven to 325°F. Line two baking sheets with parchment paper.

Whisk together the flour, baking soda, and salt in a medium bowl. Beat the brown sugar, butter, and coconut oil with an electric mixer set on high speed in a medium bowl until combined, about 1 minute. Beat in the egg, egg yolk, and vanilla. Add the peanut butter and mix well. With the mixer on low speed, mix in the flour mixture, just until combined. Stir in the chocolate chips.

Roll the dough into 30 walnut-sized balls. Arrange them about 2 inches apart on the prepared baking sheets. Using a fork, press an X into the top of each cookie, flattening it to about half of its original thickness. Refrigerate the remaining dough balls while you bake the first batch.

Bake about 20 minutes, until the cookies are golden brown. Let cool on the baking sheets for 5 minutes. Transfer to a wire cooling rack and let cool completely. Repeat with the remaining dough balls, using cooled baking sheets.

One 10.9-ounce jar cajeta

1 cup heavy cream

¼ cup whole milk

½ teaspoon instant espresso powder

Pinch of salt

2 teaspoons Kahlúa (optional)

2 pints vanilla ice cream for serving

MAKE AHEAD: The sauce will keep, covered in the refrigerator, for up to 1 week. Bring to room temperature before serving. To serve the sauce warm, heat it gently in a saucepan over low heat.

Ice Cream Sundaes with Mexican Caramel Sauce

This sauce, made with *cajeta*, is a caramel lover's dream come true. Similar to dulce de leche, which is made with cow's milk, cajeta is made with goat's milk and has a somewhat tangy flavor. Commercially made cajeta is available at Mexican markets, and it can also be purchased online. This silky sauce tastes fantastic drizzled over vanilla ice cream.

Heat water in a small saucepan over medium heat. Remove the lid from the jar of cajeta and put it in the simmering water. Let simmer for about 5 minutes to soften the consistency of the cajeta.

Scrape the cajeta into a small saucepan. Add the cream, milk, espresso powder, and salt and heat over medium-low heat, stirring constantly to prevent scorching, just until the mixture comes to a boil. Remove from the heat and stir in the Kahlúa, if using.

Pour the sauce into a medium bowl, cover with plastic wrap and let cool to room temperature (see Make Ahead).

Scoop ice cream into bowls and drizzle with the sauce.

Piñatas

Along with pin-the-tail-on-the-donkey, piñatas are considered a staple of kids' birthday parties. While today we enjoy piñatas in all shapes and sizes filled with candies and goodies, the history of the tradition is a bit more complicated.

We often associate piñatas with Mexican culture, but it's actually likely that the first "piñatas" were used in ancient Chinese New Year celebrations. Associated with the harvest, the piñatas would be shaped like oxen and decorated with symbols that were meant to bring good luck for the growing season.

In Catholic Europe, piñatas emerged as a Lenten tradition. These were made of earthenware and decorated with colorful paint, ribbons, and paper.

Now piñatas are nearly universal and employed in all kinds of celebrations including birthday parties, Christmas, and Cinco de Mayo.

1¼ cups slivered almonds

2¾ cups unbleached
all-purpose flour

1½ teaspoons baking powder

½ teaspoon kosher salt

¼ cup olive oil

3 tablespoons unsalted
butter, at room
temperature

¾ cup sugar

3 large eggs, at room
temperature

3 tablespoons fresh lemon
juice

2 teaspoons grated lemon
zest

> **MAKE AHEAD:**
> The biscotti will
> keep, covered in an
> airtight container,
> for up to 4 days.
> They can be frozen
> for up to 2 months.

Toasted Almond Biscotti

Biscotti are crunchy Italian cookies that have a subtle sweet flavor. That makes them perfect for dunking into coffee, tea, or Vin Santo, a dessert wine.

Position an oven rack in the center of the oven and preheat the oven to 350°F. Line a large baking sheet with parchment paper.

Spread the almonds out on the baking sheet and toast, stirring once, until light golden brown, about 10 minutes. Remove and let cool.

Whisk the flour, baking powder, and salt together in a medium bowl.

Using a mixer on medium speed, beat the olive oil and butter together in a large bowl. Gradually add the sugar while beating. Scrape down the sides of the bowl and beat in the eggs, one at a time, scraping the bowl after each addition. Beat in the lemon juice and zest. Stir in the flour mixture and the almonds.

Divide the dough in half. Shape each half into a long loaf, about 16-by-2-inches each. Arrange the loaves on the baking sheet.

Bake until the tops are cracked and firm, about 25 minutes. Remove and cool for 30 minutes. Reduce the oven temperature to 300°F.

Using a serrated knife, gently cut the loaves into ½-inch slices. Turn them on their sides and bake, turning once, until very lightly browned around the edges, about 40 minutes. Leave the biscotti in the oven and turn it off.

Remove the biscotti after 30 minutes and let cool completely. These taste best the day after baking (see Make Ahead).

16 ounces bittersweet or semisweet chocolate

3 cups heavy cream

2 tablespoons Kahlúa or Grand Marnier

MAKE AHEAD:
The mousse will keep, covered in the refrigerator, for up to 1 day.

Chocolate Mousse Cups

This chocolate mousse is good to serve in small glass bowls or cups for dessert when you're hosting an elegant dinner, cocktail party, or movie night. Even though it is made with just a few simple ingredients, this mousse tastes quite rich and decadent.

Combine the chocolate and ½ cup of the cream in a medium heavy saucepan and heat over very low heat, stirring frequently, until the chocolate is completely melted and smooth. Transfer to a large bowl and let cool until just barely warm.

In a large bowl, combine the remaining 2½ cups cream and the Kahlúa and using an electric mixer, beat until the cream just holds soft peaks. Do not overbeat. Add the cream to the chocolate mixture and, working quickly, fold the chocolate into the cream with a rubber spatula just until incorporated.

Transfer the mousse to a large serving bowl or individual serving dishes and refrigerate for at least an hour (see Make Ahead).

Charades

Ah, charades. Perhaps the quintessential "party" game. Actually, charades are part of a bigger tradition of what are called parlor games, having been developed in the Victorian era in Great Britain among the upper class. In fact, parlor games (from the French word for speech, parler) gave parlor rooms their name.

Want to pass the time with your friends like they did back in the day? Or finally put your Victorian-era parlor to good use? Here are some other classic parlor games to try when you're entertaining some refined society:

- Twenty Questions
- The Minster's Cat
- Murder in the Dark
- Blind Man's Buff
- Consequences
- Exquisite Corpse
- I Spy

AN AFTERNOON OF GAMES, GOOD FOOD & CONVERSATION

What could be more fun than meeting up with your fellow mahjong players or book club buddies for an afternoon of fun and games, lively conversation, and sumptuous food?

Menu

SNACKS
- Sweet & Spicy Roasted Nuts (page 16)
- Cheese Straws (page 25)
- Endive Leaves with Chicken, Walnut & Grape Salad (page 42)

MAINS
- Smoked Salmon & Cucumber Tea Sandwiches with Dill Butter (page 111)
- Egg Salad & Watercress Tea Sandwiches (page 113)

DESSERT
- Lemon Pound Cake with Fresh Berries (page 123)
- Toasted Almond Biscotti (page 143)

DRINKS
- Whiskey Sours (page 153)
- Iced Mint & Lemon Verbena Tea (page 171)

Game Plan

1 MONTH AHEAD
Bake the biscotti and freeze. Biscotti will keep in the freezer for up to 1 month.

1 WEEK AHEAD
Prepare the nuts. They will keep, covered in an airtight container, for up to 1 week.

Prepare the Cheese Straws. They will keep, covered in an airtight container, for up to 1 week.

1 DAY AHEAD
Prepare and refrigerate the chicken salad.

Bake and glaze the pound cake.

DAY OF
Prepare and refrigerate the tea sandwiches about 3 hours before serving.

Prepare and refrigerate the iced tea about 2 hours before serving.

Prepare the fruit for the cake.

Prepare the bar for the drinks.

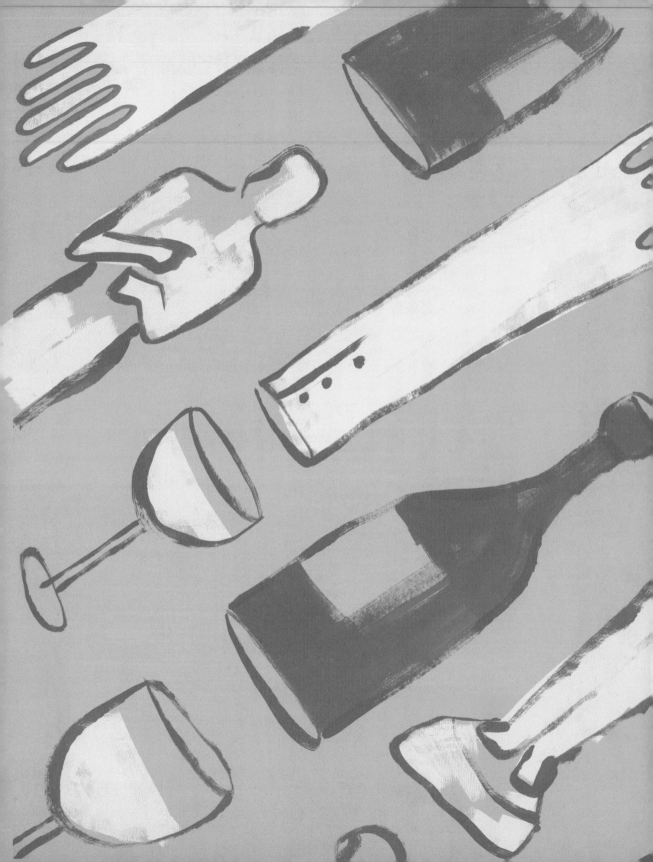

CHAPTER 5
COCKTAILS & DRINKS

Kosher salt

1 small piece of lemon, lime, or grapefruit

1½ ounces vodka

¾ ounce Campari

¾ ounce grapefruit juice, preferably fresh-squeezed

¼ ounce Simple Syrup (page 175)

Lucky Dog

This is a very refreshing drink that goes well with salty snacks like popcorn and olives. Campari may be an acquired taste for some, but it is a lovely component in this cocktail. This recipe comes from Achilles Heel, a terrific bar and restaurant in the Greenpoint neighborhood in Brooklyn, New York.

Pour the salt onto a small, shallow plate. Rub the outside of a highball glass with lemon. Dip the glass into the plate of salt to coat the rim and fill the glass with ice.

Fill a cocktail shaker with ice. Add the vodka, Campari, grapefruit juice, and simple syrup and shake vigorously. Strain into the prepared glass and serve.

Hare and Hounds

GAME FACT!

Hare and Hounds was an abstract strategy game popular in Europe in the 19th Century. Also called the French Military Game, it was especially well-liked among soldiers in France. An example of an asymmetrical game, each player controlled different pieces with different movesets.

The game is played with three hound pieces and one hare piece on a small board. From one end, the hounds charge at the hare, only able to move forward. On the other side, the hare is their prey, but is able to move both forward and backward, as well as side to side. The object of the game is for the hounds to completely trap the hare, making it so that the hare has no legal moves. The hare wins if the player passes the hounds to safely reach the other end of the board.

A game with easy-to-learn mechanics, its superficial simplicity belies its deeper complexity and potential for unique outcomes. Modern analysis shows, however, that with perfect play, it is a win for the hounds. Poor little hare.

Nor'easter Cocktail

2 ounces bourbon

½ ounce fresh lime juice

½ ounce maple syrup

1½ ounces ginger beer

Fresh lime wedge for garnish

Maple syrup is the surprise sweetener in this drink made with bourbon and lime.

Fill a cocktail shaker with ice. Add the bourbon, lime juice, and maple syrup and shake vigorously for 20 seconds. Strain into a rocks glass over fresh ice. Top off with the ginger beer, garnish with lime, and serve.

Whiskey Sour

SERVES 1

1 ounce freshly squeezed lemon juice

¾ ounce Simple Syrup (page 175)

2 ounces blended whiskey or bourbon

Orange wheel for garnish

Maraschino cherry for garnish

A whiskey sour is an old-school cocktail with a wonderful sweet and sour flavor that's just right for slow sipping on game nights. Be sure to use the freshest lemon and orange that you can find when making this drink.

Fill a cocktail shaker with ice. Add the lemon juice, simple syrup, and whiskey and shake well until very cold. Strain into an old-fashioned or rocks glass over fresh ice. Garnish with an orange wheel and a cherry and serve.

GAME FACT!

Former Olympic Sports

The modern Olympics began in 1896 and have seen many sports come and go. Sports are usually dropped from the summer and winter games because of concerns of safety or a lack of international interest in serious competition. Below are just a few of the more interesting events to be dropped from the Olympics. But because they're not sanctioned by the International Olympic Committee, it doesn't mean you can't enjoy them.

- Cricket
- Croquet
- Equestrian vaulting
- Gliding
- Lacrosse
- Offshore powerboat racing
- Polo
- Rugby

- Ski ballet
- Sled dog racing
- Speed skiing
- Tug of War
- Winter pentathlon: Cross-country skiing Shooting
- Downhill skiing
- Horse riding

2 sprigs fresh mint

½ ounce Simple Syrup (page 175)

2 ounces bourbon

Crushed ice

Mint Julep

This classic Southern cocktail is the signature drink of the Kentucky Derby. Drink it from a frosty julep cup while watching the race with your friends. The key to making a good mint julep is to use decent bourbon and very fresh mint.

In the bottom of a chilled julep cup or highball glass, gently bruise one sprig of mint with the simple syrup. Add half of the bourbon and fill halfway with crushed ice. Stir with a long spoon until the outside of the glass frosts. Add more crushed ice and the remaining bourbon to fill the glass. Stir again to frost, garnish with the remaining mint sprig and serve.

Mint Juleps and the Kentucky Derby

First run in 1875, the Kentucky Derby is one of America's oldest sporting events. In addition to being a very exciting race, it has something for everyone—sleek racing horses, tradition and pageantry, outrageous hats, and, of course, mint juleps.

A mint julep is a combination of bourbon, water, fresh mint, sugar, and crushed ice. It was a very popular drink served throughout the South in the 1800s. In partnership with Brown-Forman, a wine and spirits company based in Louisville, Kentucky, the mint julep was promoted by Churchill Downs, and in 1938 it was recognized as "the official drink of the Kentucky Derby."

Originally, the Derby's recipe was made with Early Times whiskey, but today Woodford Reserve bourbon is used in the signature drink. It is considered to be the ideal bourbon because it is very smooth with mellow caramel notes, and most importantly, it mixes well with mint and sugar.

Each year, well over 120,000 juleps are served at Churchill Downs over the two-day period of the Kentucky Oaks and the Kentucky Derby. Virtually all of them are served in specially made Kentucky Derby collectible julep cups. Although the premier race in the Kentucky Derby is billed as the fastest two minutes in sports, drinking juleps is an all-day event. The bourbon-filled cocktails are poured right after the gates open at 8 AM, and people continue imbibing all the way until last call at 8:10 PM.

SERVES 1

Crushed ice

2 ounces bourbon, preferably Woodford Reserve

1 ounce Mint Simple Syrup (page 177)

Sprig of fresh mint for garnish

Churchill Downs Mint Julep

This is the official mint julep recipe from Churchill Downs. A word here about those silver julep cups: They are not totally necessary to enjoy sipping a mint julep. Most bartenders agree that a tall highball glass is perfectly suitable.

Fill a julep cup or highball glass with crushed ice. Pour the bourbon and simple syrup over it and stir with a spoon. Garnish with a fresh sprig of mint.

6 ounces cold beer

6 ounces lemonade, preferably Homemade Lemonade (page 166)

Lemon wheel for garnish

Beer & Lemonade Shandy

A shandy is simply a combination of equal parts beer and lemonade. It is immensely refreshing, and it couldn't be easier to make. It is best to make it with a light beer like a wheat beer, light lager, or a pilsner. When you make this drink, you can use store-bought lemonade, but it is fantastic with homemade lemonade.

Fill a standard pint glass halfway with beer and top it off with lemonade. Garnish with a lemon wheel and serve.

Michelada

SERVES 1

Celery salt for rimming the glass

Chile lime seasoning for rimming the glass

2 lime wedges

6 dashes hot sauce, such as Cholula or Valentina

4 ounces Clamato juice

4 dashes Worcestershire sauce

1 ounce fresh lime juice

One 12-ounce can or bottle of Mexican beer, such as Modelo, Sol, or Tecate

When making a michelada, be sure to seek out chile lime seasoning for rimming the glass. It adds a nice kick to the drink. Chile lime seasoning is available in the spice sections of supermarkets, Trader Joe's, and online.

Combine the celery salt and chile lime seasoning on a small, shallow plate. Rub the rim of a chilled pint glass with one of the lime wedges and dip the glass into the mixture. Coat the inside of the glass with the hot sauce and fill with ice cubes.

Add the Clamato juice, Worcestershire sauce, and lime juice. Stir and top off with the beer. Garnish with the remaining lime wedge and serve with the remaining beer to top off as you drink.

BATCH IT!

Mix together the Clamato juice, Worcestershire sauce, and lime juice in a pitcher for the desired total serving amount. Cover and refrigerate for a few hours or overnight. Shake well before serving each drink in a prepared glass with the beer.

1 ounce crème de cassis

4 ounces champagne

1 lemon twist for garnish

Kir Royale

Crème de cassis is a black currant–flavored liqueur that is produced in Burgundy, France. It is an essential ingredient in a kir (made with white wine) or kir royale (made with champagne).

Pour the crème de cassis into a champagne flute and add champagne to fill. Stir gently to combine. Garnish with the lemon twist and serve.

BATCH IT! If you're making a batch of drinks with champagne, prosecco, cava, or any other sparkling wine, a good rule of thumb is that two 750 ml bottles will make 10 drinks, four bottles will make 20, and so on.

Foosball

Foosball, or table soccer, is generally played for fun in bars and basements all over the world. But there are some folks who take the game a bit more seriously and really push it to its limits. For example, Italian artist Maurizio Cattelan created a foosball table that runs seven meters long and accommodates 11 players to a side, so two full soccer teams can play. Called *Stadium*, the piece sold at a Sotheby's auction in 2013 for $2,629,000—a bit more than what the local pub paid for theirs.

Based in France, the International Table Soccer Federation is the international governing body of serious foosball competitions, including the bi-annual World Cup.

Sangria with Peaches & Strawberries

SYRUP

1 cup sugar

½ cup water

Zest of 1 orange

Zest of 1 lemon

1 cinnamon stick

SANGRIA

One bottle (750 ml)
full-bodied red wine,
such as Côtes du Rhône

¼ cup brandy

½ orange, thinly sliced

½ lemon, thinly sliced

1 peach, peeled, pitted, and
thinly sliced

8 fresh strawberries, hulled
and halved

This delicious summery sangria is made with a syrup that is infused with lemon and orange zest. Add red wine, brandy, and fresh fruit, serve over lots of ice, and you're good to go.

TO MAKE THE SYRUP: Mix together the sugar, water, orange zest, and lemon zest in a saucepan and bring to a boil over high heat. Reduce the heat, add the cinnamon stick, and simmer, stirring with a wooden spoon, for about 5 minutes, until the sugar dissolves. Strain into a lidded glass jar or similar container. Discard the cinnamon stick. Cool, cover, and refrigerate (see Make Ahead).

TO MAKE THE SANGRIA: Pour the wine, brandy, and ¼ cup of the syrup into a pitcher; reserve the remaining syrup for later batches of sangria. Add the orange, lemon, and peach slices, and the strawberries and stir. Cover and refrigerate for 2 to 3 hours, or until ready to serve. Pour over ice in tall glasses.

MAKE AHEAD:
The syrup will keep,
covered in the
refrigerator, for
1 day.

Ginger-Lime Fizz

SERVES 1

6 ounces ginger beer

1 tablespoon Ginger Simple Syrup (page 176)

1 tablespoon fresh lime juice

Splash of sparkling water

Lime wedge for garnish

The combination of ginger beer and lime really makes this drink shine. If you want to spike it, add a shot of vodka or bourbon.

Fill a rocks glass with ice. Add the ginger beer, ginger simple syrup, and lime juice and stir. Top off with sparkling water, garnish with a lime wedge, and serve.

1 cup freshly squeezed lemon juice (8 to 1o lemons)

1 cup sugar

6 cups of cold water

Lemon slices for garnish

Homemade Lemonade

There are so many things that taste better made from scratch, and homemade lemonade is at the top of the list. This recipe uses only lemons, sugar, and water. It's a good one that you will use again and again.

Strain the lemon juice through a fine-mesh strainer into a large measuring cup or bowl. Add the sugar to the lemon juice and whisk until the sugar is completely dissolved.

Transfer the lemonade base to a large serving pitcher. Add the water and stir well to combine. Chill the lemonade for at least 1 hour before serving. Pour over ice in tall glasses, garnish with lemon slices, and serve.

1 cup sugar

½ cup water

1½ cups freshly squeezed lime juice (12 to 14 limes)

1½ liters (6 cups) of club soda or seltzer

Lime slices for garnish

Sparkling Limeade

Limeade is an excellent thirst quencher to serve on warm afternoons or evenings. It tastes terrific on its own, or add a shot of tequila or rum for a lively cocktail.

Mix together the sugar and water in a saucepan and bring to a boil over high heat. Reduce the heat and simmer, stirring with a wooden spoon until the sugar dissolves, about 5 minutes. Strain into a lidded glass jar or similar container. Let cool, cover, and refrigerate.

Pour the lime juice into a large pitcher. Add about ¾ cup of the sugar mixture, or more to taste. Reserve any remaining mixture for another batch of limeade. Stir well and pour over ice in tall glasses. Add club soda to fill the glasses and stir gently. Garnish with lime slices and serve.

4 cups freshly chopped fruit

3 cups cold water

1 to 2 tablespoons sugar or maple syrup

1 lime, juiced

Fresh mint leaves for garnish

MAKE AHEAD:
If not serving immediately, the agua fresca will keep, covered in the refrigerator, for up to 3 days. Stir well before serving.

Agua Fresca

Agua fresca (fresh water) is a refreshing fruit drink that's very easy to make at home. To make this drink, all you need is chopped fruit, water, sugar, and a blender. Watermelon is one of the most popular fruits for agua fresca, but there are plenty of other good options. Try making it with some other sweet fruits, such as honeydew melon, cantaloupe, pineapple, papaya, or strawberries.

Put the fruit, water, sugar, and lime juice in a blender and blend until completely smooth. Taste and adjust the flavor, if necessary. Strain the mixture through a fine mesh sieve into a large pitcher (see Make Ahead).

Pour into large glasses filled with ice, garnish with mint leaves, and serve.

2 quarts water

3 tablespoons orange pekoe
    tea leaves

½ cup sugar

2 tablespoons fresh sliced
    ginger

1 stick cinnamon

Orange slices for garnish

Iced Orange & Ginger Tea

Homemade iced tea made with orange pekoe leaves and fresh ginger is much better than any instant or store-bought tea. This is a good drink to serve to your thirsty guests along with a slice of cake or some cookies.

Bring the water to a full boil in a large saucepan. Add the tea, sugar, ginger, and cinnamon stick and remove the pan from the heat. Cover and let stand for 5 minutes. Stir gently to dissolve the sugar. Let stand for 5 minutes longer.

Strain the tea into a pitcher and let cool to room temperature. Refrigerate for at least 2 hours. Pour over ice in chilled glasses, garnish with orange slices, and serve.

2 quarts water

2 tablespoons mint tea leaves

1 tablespoon plus 1 teaspoon clover honey

8 sprigs lemon verbena

Lemon slices for garnish

Iced Mint & Lemon Verbena Tea

Lemon verbena is a perennial shrub with leaves that have a distinctive lovely lemon scent. These leaves are often used for making tea and potpourri. In this recipe, sprigs of lemon verbena are steeped in hot water along with mint tea leaves and honey to create an amazing and restorative iced tea.

Bring the water to a full boil in a large saucepan. Add the tea and remove the pan from the heat. Cover and let stand for 5 minutes. Add the honey and stir until dissolved. Add the lemon verbena sprigs and let stand for 5 more minutes.

Strain the tea into a pitcher and let cool to room temperature. Refrigerate for at least 2 hours. Pour over ice in chilled glasses, garnish with lemon slices, and serve.

Fruit Smoothies

Smoothies are simply a blend of fresh fruit and yogurt (and maybe a bit of honey or vanilla). They can be whipped up in a blender on a moment's notice and are good energy boosters for both kids and grown-ups.

SERVES 1

6 ounces (⅔ cup) low-fat vanilla yogurt

½ cup ice cubes

¼ cup fresh blueberries, plus more for garnish

BLUEBERRY SMOOTHIE

Put the yogurt, ice cubes, and blueberries in a blender. Blend on high until the ice cubes are crushed and the consistency is smooth.

Pour into a glass, garnish with fresh blueberries, and serve at once.

BANANA SMOOTHIE

SERVES 1

2 tablespoons honey

½ teaspoon pure vanilla extract

1 ripe banana, sliced

6 ounces (⅔ cup) plain yogurt

½ cup ice

Put the honey, vanilla, banana, yogurt, and ice in a blender and blend, gradually increasing the speed until the mixture is smooth.

Pour the drink into a chilled glass and serve at once.

European Playing Cards

While we're accustomed to spades, hearts, clubs, and diamonds, derived from the French deck, playing cards from other countries offer many other styles of suits. Germany, Italy, Spain, and Switzerland have unique decks that also feature some differences in the face cards.

Italian and Spanish

SUITS

- Swords
- Cups
- Coins
- Batons

FACE CARDS

- Knave
- Knight
- King

German

SUITS

- Acorns
- Leaves
- Hearts
- Bells

FACE CARDS

- Underling
- Officer
- King

Swiss

SUITS

- Bells
- Shields
- Roses
- Acorns

FACE CARDS

- Fool
- Clerk
- King

1 cup sugar

1 cup water

Simple Syrup

Simple syrup is a mixture of sugar and water, and it is an important addition to all kinds of drinks. It's very easy to prepare and keeps well, and it's always good to have some on hand in the refrigerator. Most simple syrup recipes call for one part sugar to one part water, but feel free to experiment with different ratios (see below) to come up with your preferred version.

Put the sugar and water in a small saucepan and bring to a gentle boil over medium-high heat, stirring to dissolve the sugar. Reduce the heat and simmer, stirring occasionally, until the sugar is completely dissolved and the syrup is slightly thickened, about 3 minutes.

Remove from the heat and let cool. Transfer the syrup to a container with a tight-fitting lid; cover and refrigerate until ready to use. The syrup will keep, covered in the refrigerator, for up to 3 or 4 weeks.

Simple Syrup Ratios: Here are some standard ratio variations.

- Thick simple syrup: 1 part water to 1 part sugar

- Medium simple syrup: 2 parts water to 1 part sugar

- Thin simple syrup: 3 parts water to 1 part sugar

1 cup of sugar

½ cup water

Four 1-inch pieces fresh
   ginger, trimmed and peeled

Ginger Simple Syrup

Fresh ginger adds a nice aromatic kick to a simple syrup. It blends beautifully with lemonade and iced tea as well as bourbon and whiskey.

Put the sugar, water, and ginger in a small saucepan and stir. Bring to a gentle boil over medium-high heat. Reduce the heat and simmer, stirring occasionally, until the sugar is completely dissolved and the syrup is slightly thickened, about 3 minutes.

Remove from the heat and let cool. Strain the syrup into a container with a tight-fitting lid; cover and refrigerate until ready to use. The syrup will keep, covered in the refrigerator, for up to 2 weeks.

½ cup sugar

1 cup water

½ cup fresh mint leaves

Mint Simple Syrup

A mint simple syrup is often used in mint juleps, but it is also a very flavorful addition to cold drinks such as lemonade and iced tea.

Put the sugar and water in a small saucepan and stir. Bring to a boil over medium-high heat, stirring to dissolve the sugar. Add the mint leaves. Reduce the heat to a simmer and cook, without stirring, until the syrup is slightly thickened, about 10 minutes.

Remove from the heat and let cool. Strain the syrup into a container with a tight-fitting lid, discarding the mint leaves. Cover and refrigerate until ready to use. The syrup will keep, covered in the refrigerator, for up to 4 weeks.

Mancala

The Mancala family of games represent perhaps the oldest game in civilization. A precursor to games like backgammon, ludo, and the Royal Game of Ur, Mancala is played by moving stones from your side of the board across your opponent's side and then finally off the board or "home." Mancala games are two-player games of abstract strategy and are still widely played today in many different variations. They are especially popular in Southeast Asia and Africa with different traditional styles of board.

However, the earliest Mancala games weren't played on boards at all. Instead, historians say that prehistoric civilizations dug small holes into the earth, typically four to eight per player. These were often improvised, temporary play setups, although some more permanent Mancala holes have been discovered. As far as the tokens, people would play with whatever small implements were in their surroundings, usually rocks, seeds, or animal bones and teeth.

Today, most commercial Mancala sets are made of wood and come with glass stones. Still, you don't need to spend a dime to play the game. Just draw some circles on paper and play with coins or beans. Or take it outside and dig your own Mancala playing pit!

Tarot

Though our primary association with tarot cards might be ancient mysticism, divination and cartomancy, the deck was actually probably invented in Italy in the 15th century. The tarot deck emerged in Europe around the same time as other playing cards, inspired by cards from Egypt. The tarot deck's original purpose was to play games. Popular ones included the Italian tarocchini and the French tarot. It wasn't until the late 1700s that esotericisits began to use tarot decks for occult practices and fortune-telling. But, if you wish to indulge in a bit of fantasy, here's a simple guide to the popular associations with the various suits and major arcana to be found in the deck. Nothing wrong with a quick psychic reading before dessert!

Suit of Wands: Element of fire, primal energy, creativity, and passion

Suit of Pentacles: Element of earth, material world, growth, and money

Suit of Swords: Element of air, action, power, and courage

Suit of Cups: Element of water, imagination, relationships, and healing

Major Arcana:

0 Fool
—New beginnings

I Magician
—Inspiration

II High Priestess
—Intuition

III Empress
—Nurturing

IV Emperor
—Authority

V Hierophant
—Spirituality

VI Lovers
—Harmony

VII Chariot
—Determination

VIII Strength
—Willpower

IX Hermit
—Introspection

X Wheel of Fortune
—Luck

XI Justice
—Fairness

XII The Hanged Man
—Surrender

XIII Death
—Endings

XIV Temperance
—Moderation

XV Devil
—Attachment

XVI The Tower
—Chaos

XVII The Star
—Hope

XVIII The Moon
—Fear

XIX The Sun
—Vitality

XX Judgement
—Absolution

XXI The World
—Completion

How to Set Up a Home Bar

Even if you're not an expert mixologist, it's a good idea to set up a home bar for times when you want to make a proper cocktail for yourself and your guests.

Here is a list of spirits and mixers that you will need for a well-stocked bar at home. This can be expensive to do all at once, so you can build your bar a bottle at a time.

Clear Spirits
- Vodka
- Gin
- Tequila
- White rum

Brown Spirits
- Whiskey
  - Bourbon
  - Rye
  - Scotch
- Dark rum

Aperitifs
- Campari
- Aperol

Additions
- Vermouth
- Bitters

Sparkling Wine
- Champagne
- Prosecco
- Cava

Mixers
- Soda water
- Tonic
- Ginger beer
- Sodas
- Fresh juices

Garnishes
- Fresh lemons and limes
- Fresh mint
- Cocktail olives
- Cocktail onions
- Horseradish
- Hot sauce

Equipment
- Cocktail shaker
- Jigger
- Bar spoon
- Strainer
- Corkscrew

A SWANKY EVENING AT HOME COCKTAIL PARTY

There are times when no other type of gathering will do except for a swanky cocktail party. Whether you are celebrating a special birthday or anniversary or hosting an Oscar party, it's fun to dress up and serve an array of scrumptious hors d'oeuvres and festive cocktails. Be sure to give yourself enough time so that you can make your food look beautiful and inviting.

Menu

SNACKS
- Cucumber Rounds with Whipped Cream Cheese & Smoked Salmon (page 30)
- Ginger Shrimp Cocktail with Thai Dipping Sauce (page 41)
- Ham & Cheese Mini Quiches (page 43)
- Grilled Lemon-Rosemary Chicken Skewers (page 46)

DESSERT
- Chocolate Mousse Cups (page 144)
- Luscious Lemon Wafers (page 133)

DRINKS
- Kir Royales (page 160)
- Sparkling Limeade (page 167)

Game Plan

1 MONTH AHEAD
Prepare and freeze the dough for mini quiches for up to 1 month.

3 DAYS AHEAD
Bake the lemon wafers. They will keep, in an airtight container, for up to 3 days.

2 DAYS AHEAD
Prepare and refrigerate the whipped cream cheese.

Prepare and refrigerate the Thai dipping sauce.

1 DAY AHEAD
Prepare and refrigerate the chocolate mousse.

Prepare and refrigerate the shrimp.

Prepare and refrigerate the limeade.

DAY OF
Prepare and bake the mini quiches. Serve warm or at room temperature.

Assemble the cucumber rounds about 1 hour before serving.

Grill or bake the chicken skewers shortly before serving.

Prepare the bar for drinks.

ACKNOWLEDGMENTS

Many thanks to the people at The Countryman Press: Michael Tizzano, for making this project happen; Ann Treistman and Isabel McCarthy, for their solid editorial support and for seeing this book through to the end with great care; and Allison Chi, for her invaluable design vision and production expertise.

A huge thank you to Jamie Runnells for her beautiful, witty illustrations and for being such a pleasure to work with. Thanks also to my agent, Eryn Kalavsky.

Thanks especially to my "little family"—Lester, Zan, and Isabelle—for their love, support, and everything else.

INDEX